Real Life Organizing

Clean and Clutter-Free in 15 Minutes a Day

Cassandra Aarssen

Contents

Foreword

Peter Walsh
Bestselling Author

Chances are you're leafing through the pages of this book, wondering whether to buy it and wondering even more about how to successfully tackle that clutter you're struggling with.

Everyone struggles with clutter to some degree, and all of us can use a little help with being more organized. That's where Cas Aarssen comes in! Here in *Real Life Organizing* is a real solution to the clutter challenges we all face. A real solution from a real mom, and parent, and homeowner, and career person who knows what it is to struggle and to overcome disorganization in all its forms.

I've worked for the past fifteen years helping people get their whole lives organized and I firmly believe that our homes are metaphors for our lives – they tell our story and show the world who we are. I believe it's impossible to make your best choices, your most enlightened, spiritually rich, emotionally stable choices in a cluttered and disorganized home. It just can't happen. Time and time again, I have seen how clutter hurts families and have witnessed firsthand, again and again, that when you declutter and open a space you create the opportunity for amazing things to flow into that space.

Real Life Organizing leads you through the sometimes-difficult, always-rewarding path of decluttering your home. By identifying your 'clutter' style you are helped to determine the best way forward. This, combined with sensible and achievable tips and techniques, enables anyone to tackle clutter, organize spaces and find the peace and harmony that every family deserves.

Stuff has power, and the stuff we own has power—power for good or power for ill. It's up to each of us to decide how we use the stuff we own. Once again, this is where Cas steps in. Not only does she help the reader understand the power of what they own, she also helps them to see their stuff as tools to help them create the life they want. The words "organization" and "organic" have the same root that means whole, complete, one. And that is the transformative power of organizing a home.

Real Life Organizing is a reflection of so much of the wonderful work Cas does on her YouTube channel and elsewhere. She demonstrates in these pages that organizing doesn't have to be the impossible or overwhelming task that many think. By establishing routines, implementing simple systems and making organization part of your daily life you can conquer clutter once and for all!

Organization is not something you do, it's the way you live your life. It is not about simply cleaning up, it is about making mindful decisions everyday about your life. *Real Life Organizing* will help with all that – and more!

YOU HAVE ENOUGH

YOU DO ENOUGH

YOU ARE ENOUGH

RELAX

Introduction

I feel it necessary to, right from the start, give you a disclaimer regarding this book. While I am in fact a Professional Organizer and I do make my living organizing other people's homes, teaching college workshops on organization and creating weekly YouTube videos and blog posts offering organizing tips… **I am a crazy, unorganized, giant disaster on the inside.**

I AM NOT a naturally organized person. In fact, the majority of my life has been spent living as a complete and utter super slob.

Want some examples of my extreme slobiness? Brace yourself. In my early twenties, I was at the height of my all time mess making. I was working three jobs and cleaning my apartment wasn't high on my priority list. My fridge got so bad that I decided to try and mask the putrid smell with Pine-Sol. Note: DO NOT POUR PINE-SOL IN YOUR FRIDGE AND LEAVE IT THERE. The only thing this did was make everything smell, and taste like artificial pine trees….for months.

I also threw out an obnoxious amount of pots and pans because weeks of caked on grime seemed so daunting that it was easier to just buy new ones. I eventually switched over entirely to paper plates and plastic cutlery too. Did I mention the piles of dirty clothes that covered almost every square inch of my floor? I had literal paths carved into them so I could walk from one room into the next. I'm making you feel like Martha Stewart right about now, aren't I?

Was I lazy? Of course I was. Am I still lazy? Absolutely! The only difference is that now I have discovered easy and inexpensive tips, tricks, and solutions that allow me to have a clean, organized, and functional home with minimal effort to maintain it. I have gone out of my way to find and create solutions that make my home seem almost self-cleaning; I have way more important things to do than spend my time cleaning up all day long, like binge watching Netflix! My point is, if I can have a clean and clutter-free home, you can certainly have one, too.

I have read dozens of amazing books on home organization. I would wager a bet that I have pretty much read every book ever written on the subject, as organizing has become my most favorite hobby (obsession). I am constantly on the hunt for new and unique ways to make my life easier (a.k.a allow me to be even lazier). I have organized my own home, clients' homes, and spent the past seven years dedicating myself to learning as much as I possibly can about how best to have a clean, clutter-free and functional home with the least amount of effort to maintain it. I wanted to put together this book and share the very best advice I have learned for real life organizing for real people with kids and pets—and, well, just a whole lot of stuff.

So here is how my organizing journey began. After we had our first daughter, Isabelle (Izzy), I was adamant that I would stay home with her full time, so I started a daycare from my house. When I say I "started a daycare," what I mean is I first tried everything I could think of to earn money while being a stay at home parent, and when all of those ideas failed miserably, the idea of babysitting other children seemed like my only viable option. One morning I randomly placed an advertisement offering childcare services online and handed out a few flyers in our neighbourhood (no thought or organization was put into this venture). In just a few short days, after dozens of calls from neighbourhood parents, I was running a home daycare just like that. At

one point, I was watching nine children… nine! My life and my home were filled with brightly colored toys, loud screaming children, and absolute chaos. This last minute career option turned out to be more amazing than I could ever have hoped for. I was able to be home with my children and they were able to have wonderful friends each and everyday to play with. Being a daycare provider helped me to become the best parent I could be. I spent my days singing songs, doing crafts, and playing games with my children (there was also a lot of snot… and poop).

Running a daycare from our tiny home came at a price, though. Our home had little storage and was bursting with toys, games, craft supplies, and endless amounts of baby stuff. Why do such tiny babies need soooo much stuff?

By this time in my life, I had the kind of home that looked somewhat tidy in the main living areas, but opening closets was like playing Russian Roulette; there was a very good chance you would be impaled with falling objects as soon as you opened the door. Every closet, every drawer, and every spot that was out of sight was jammed full of random, hidden junk. We actually had drawers so stuffed they couldn't even open, so they remained stuffed, wasted space in my kitchen.

Everyday was a hunt for something. I used to swear that someone must have broken into our home and stolen random things because, for the life of me, I just could not find anything when I needed it. As irrational as I knew it was, I would freak out and insist that someone must have broken into our house and stolen random, inexpensive stuff because there was no way that it had completely vanished into thin air. Umbrellas, shoes, bottle openers, jackets... every single day something would go missing and I would have to tear the house apart looking for it. Once I was done, I would literally shove everything back into whichever hole I had dragged it out of or wherever I could make it fit.

After our second daughter, Abigail (Abby) was born, our tiny 900-square-foot home was bursting at the seams and a complete and total disaster. Adding another baby to the mix just made my life even more hectic and created even more mess. My days were filled with cleaning up after both the daycare kids and my own kids. I would fall into bed each night overwhelmed, exhausted and dreading the next morning, when I would have to get up and do it all over again. **I felt as though I was always cleaning and tidying, yet nothing ever got clean or tidy!**

Let's fast forward to today. My third child, Miles (Milo), is almost four years old, and despite our hectic daily schedules filled with work, school, and extracurricular activities every night of the week, **we have more free time than ever.** Our house is clean and clutter-free **all of the time** and I spend less than thirty minutes a day keeping it that way. **Gone are the days of being a slave to housework.** Also gone are the days of having to search endlessly for lost items. I can honestly say that I cannot remember the last time anyone in our home has misplaced anything. I am less stressed, getting far more accomplished, and I have more time to spend doing the things I love than I ever had before.

So what changed? How did I transform from a frazzled and exhausted super slob into a relaxed and happy clean freak? I organized my home. I didn't just clean out a closet one afternoon and make it look pretty; I found systems that allow me and my family to easily find and put away everything in our home. Your organizational systems have to be so easy and effortless that everyone in your family can use it, without even realizing that they are.

I began my journey with organization through trial and error. I started with just one drawer, one shelf or some other small area at a time. Every time I would organize a new space in my home, I would see immediate, dramatic, and long lasting results. After organizing and reorganizing toys in vain for years, I realized the systems that I was using were just totally ineffective for little kids. I created a new method that enabled my daycare kids to clean up the toys themselves and have it stay organized and tidy all the time. The changes in my home were so addicting that organizing everything I could soon became my favorite hobby.

I started videoing myself doing different organizing projects and I was so excited about how life changing it was, I began posting these videos on YouTube. To my utter amazement, my YouTube channel started to grow and families in my community began reaching out to me to organize their homes as well. Soon, solely through word of mouth, my client base and YouTube channel continued to grow, and I found myself teaching organizing workshops at our local college, giving interviews on local news stations, and even appearing multiple times on a national television show offering my organizing tips and advice. Freaking crazy pants, right? How did I, a total slob, become someone who makes their living giving organizing advice?

I used to say that I "fell" into my career as an "Organizing Expert," and while that is somewhat true, I think a better explanation is that I "fell in love" with organization. It is the only thing I have ever discovered that can give you immediate and long lasting results from just fifteen minutes of effort. **You can spend just fifteen minutes organizing a drawer and have it instantly make your life easier and save you time each and everyday that you use it.** If I could spend just fifteen minutes on the treadmill and see the same immediate and long-lasting results, I'd be a size two! **Nothing else can compare to the instant gratification and long-last results (with such little time and effort invested) as organization.**

Do I still forget my kid's bathing suits when we go to pool parties? Sometimes. Am I some perfect Stepford wife who has everything under control? Not even close! I am still the same, total disaster on the inside.

My husband now calls me "the messiest clean person" he has ever met. Do I still destroy the counter when I make a sandwich? You betcha! Does the bathroom look like a hurricane came through every morning after I get ready? Of course! The difference is that now it takes me less than one minute to put everything away when I am done. I've identified my natural tendencies (I'm lazy and I like to hide things) and I created organizing systems to work with those tendencies in order to make tidying up fast and easy.

You *can* organize your closet and have it stay organized for good! If you have struggled with organization in the past, let me assure you that it is not your fault and that you can transform your home and have it stay that way for good. The secret to really, truly getting organized and staying organized for life is to first understand your organizing style, learn tricks and tips to make organizing effortless, and learning painless techniques to help you let go of your clutter.

In this book, we will start from the beginning and I will walk you through the steps you need to create a beautiful, organized, and almost self-cleaning home. You don't have to get rid of all of your things, you don't have to be a yoga-loving minimalist, and you don't have to radically change your lifestyle or personality in order to have an organized home. I am proof that you do not need to be an organized person to live like an organized person.

CHAPTER ONE

What ClutterBug are You?

While on my journey from **Cluttered to Clean**, I realized that **not all organizing systems work for all people.** I would watch organizing shows on HGTV and copy the beautifully stacked, matching bin systems in my own closet, only to have it look like a bomb went off a week later. I remember asking myself all the time, why can't I get my home together?

The reason I was struggling was because my brain doesn't work like those organizers I see on TV. I have a natural tendency to organize things a certain way and not every system or product is made to work with my style. I also discovered that most of my clients organized differently as well; some of them like to see all of their belongings out all of the time. They would claim "out of sight, out of mind," which was the exact opposite of how I organized. Some clients were meticulous pilers, perfectionists even. They would

"wait" to put away their belongings until they had the time to do it "right."

The most important thing I have learned during my journey towards living a cleaner and clutter-free lifestyle is that having an organized home isn't about having a beautiful or Pinterest-worthy space. An organized home doesn't necessarily mean a perfect home, and it certainly doesn't include spending a lot of money or endless amounts of time to make it look like a magazine spread. Being truly organized is about making things so functional and easy to use that you are able to save time, save money, and enjoy a household that practically runs itself. Sometimes, the most efficient way to organize your space isn't necessarily what works the best for someone else's home. **Organizing is not one size fits all.**

Once I finally realized that copying beautiful organizing systems from Pinterest, television, or magazines wasn't going to actually keep me organized, I started finding solutions that worked for my unique organizing style, my unique space, and my very unique family.

After countless attempts to organize the hundreds of toys played with everyday in my home daycare, it occurred to me that perhaps the reason the toys were never staying organized had less to do with the fact that children are walking disaster zones and more to do with the fact that I had not given them an organizing system that was easy and effective for them to use all by themselves.

I had purchased dozens of different plastic storage containers in all shapes and sizes, and I even packed away all of the messiest toy offenders, like the dreaded feet impaling Lego. Despite all of my best efforts, the mess remained. Every night I would spend an hour picking up all of the toys, and just a few hours into the next morning, the playroom would be a heap of brightly colored toys once again.

The only toys the children seemed able to really pick up and put away properly all by themselves were the ones that they could literally throw and toss back into the container, without much effort.

This was the first aha moment for me when it came to understanding different organizing styles and how to use those styles to develop systems that actually worked. I realized little kids just don't clean the same way I did, and therefore they would need a specific system that works for the way they think and clean up.

As I started working to organize the homes of clients and friends and family, I began to notice and keep track of the unique ways each of them organized and cleaned their homes. **There seemed to be four really distinct organizing styles, and I could soon fit everyone I knew into one of these four categories, which I called "ClutterBugs".**

Of course there is a bit of overlap, but for the most part, each person really does have a tendency to need their items organized a certain way, and once that way is identified, it is easier to create a system that will work long term for that person and their family.

Now that I understand my husband's organizing style, I can appreciate why he has countless stacks of neatly piled papers always on his desk (I can appreciate it, not like it), and I can help him create efficient ways to deal with paper. When I visit my sister's home, I understand her need to "see" everything she has and her fear that if she puts important things away, she will forget about them and they will be lost forever. I am also now completely aware of my own tendency to "hide and shove" things into hidden areas in my home, and I can create systems that allow me to continue to hide and shove, but in a more organized way.

Discovering your own unique style is like a light bulb moment! You will be able to see what systems can work best for you and why certain systems will never work for you. Armed with this new knowledge, you will be able to create real-life systems and solutions and an organizing game plan that will transform your home and your life forever.

So, what's your organizing style? Take the following test to find out!

Note: When taking this test, try to think about your own personal spaces inside your home and how you personally deal with your belongings. When living with different people, the state of our current home can be a reflection of all of those styles combined. Try to answer this test objectively and from your own personal point of view.

You enjoy reading a:

1. Magazine or Comic Book
2. Non-Fiction Book
3. Fiction Book
4. Newspaper

You find your biggest clutter issue is:

1. I have "stuff" everywhere
2. Paper and other personal or important items
3. Inside closets, cabinets, and spare rooms
4. I hold on to too many things that may be useful in the future

Your home usually looks:

1. Cluttered with random things everywhere
2. Tidy with occasional piles of papers or things I haven't got to yet
3. Very clean and tidy, but behind closed doors, closets and drawers can be a mess
4. A bit cluttered with projects or items I am still using in some areas

In my spare time I enjoy:

1. Visiting with friends or family outside of my home
2. Learning, reading, or trying something new
3. Relaxing in my home
4. Enjoying my favorite hobbies

The areas in your home that need the most organizing are:

1. Bedrooms, kitchen, and just about everywhere else
2. Desk, filing systems, and office
3. Closets, drawers, storage rooms and spare bedrooms
4. Work areas like kitchen, craft rooms, and garage

When it comes to cleaning my home I generally:

1. Always have to spend a lot of time tidying up before I can clean it
2. Keep my home clean and tidy, but it isn't a priority in my life
3. Have a pretty clean house and I enjoy cleaning it
4. Clean it sometimes, but some areas are always pretty cluttered

My biggest organizing challenge is:

1. Out of sight is out of mind, so I tend to leave everything out all the time
2. I just haven't scheduled time to organize some areas efficiently
3. I tend to neglect hidden areas in my home, like storage rooms
4. I hate putting things away that I am just going to take out again later

If a friend called and said she would be coming over in ten minutes, you would:

1. Make a mad-dash grabbing as much clutter as you could and storing it out of sight
2. Not do much differently
3. Wipe counters and scrub the bathrooms in a hurry
4. Finish up whatever it was you were working on

When I am anxious, I:

1. Talk it over in my head or speak with close friends and family
2. Try to analyze and mentally prepare for all scenarios
3. Worry and get myself worked up
4. Distract myself with hobbies or work

I remember things best from:

1. Visual pictures and instructions
2. Reading and researching about it
3. Someone showing me how to do it
4. Figuring it out on my own

My excuse for not organizing my home is:

1. There is so much clutter that I am overwhelmed and don't know where to start
2. I am a bit of a perfectionist, so organizing takes a long time to do it right
3. No one except for our family can see all of my hidden messy areas, so why bother
4. I'm always busy with projects and hobbies and I do not have the time

I like my favorite things to be:

1. Out where I can always see them or else they may get lost
2. Stored or displayed properly so that they will last
3. Neat and tidy and displayed in an eye-pleasing way
4. Where I can easily use them often

I like to decorate my home:

1. With bold colors and artwork
2. With minimal, neutral colors
3. With current design trends
4. With useful, functional pieces

I would like my home to be:

1. Fun and Bright
2. Functional and Minimal
3. Beautiful and Cozy
4. Practical and Efficient

What is your Organizing Style?

Add up your answers. Are you mostly a 1, 2, 3 or 4? You may also be a combination of all of these organizing styles! Below are descriptions of each style and some tips and tricks that can help you finally get and stay organized!

What Clutterbug Are You?

If you answered mostly **1**, you are a **BUTTERFLY**!

If you answered mostly **2**, you are a **CRICKET**!

If you answered mostly **3**, you are a **LADYBUG**!

If you answered mostly **4**, you are a **BEE**!

Note: There is, in fact, a fifth "ClutterBug," the rare and amazing "Dragonfly." A Dragonfly is an incredibly organized person who is usually an extreme minimalist and rarely, if ever, struggles with clutter or mess. We hate Dragonflies. If you are a Dragonfly, you can stop reading this book now—I will have nothing more to offer you!

BUTTERFLY

A Butterfly is a very visual person and generally likes to see all their belongings for fear of **"out of sight, out of mind."** While almost all ClutterBugs need to have some important papers or reminders in plain sight in order to remember them, Butterflies take this to an extreme and struggle to put things "away" when they are done using them. Unfortunately, it just isn't feasible to leave all of our things out all of the time. **You are probably a Butterfly if you have clothing on top of your dresser and on the floor, but your closet and drawers are practically empty.**

Butterflies are often overwhelmed with the idea of organizing, have no idea where to begin, and therefore put off starting big organizing projects. They also can become easily distracted and can float like a "butterfly" from task to task without really completing any of the projects that they begin. A Butterfly has to be careful not to overrun their home with clutter which can steal their time, energy and can have a negative impact of those they love.

With all of that being said, Butterflies are almost always fun, artistic, creative individuals who, once their space is organized in a way that works for their style, can take immense pride in making their home a beautiful and inspiring retreat for themselves and their family.

There are many ways a Butterfly can be organized with everything in its place, without the fear of forgetting where something is. Here are some quick tips just for Butterflies:

- Brightly colored or clear bins are perfect for you and can motivate you to put your things away! Keep the lids off, though, so you are more likely to use them. By keeping your organizing solutions clear or colorful, you will be much more likely to use them and it will be a visual reminder of where your items are! Consider red bins for crafts, blue for office supplies, or all clear bins so you can always see what is inside.

- Label, label, label. Labeling is magic and every bug should do this, but it is most important for Butterflies and Crickets. You can use word or pictures to label your bins and baskets so you always have a visual reminder of what is inside. Use clearly labeled baskets for mail, clothing, office supplies, paperwork and just about everything else. There have been numerous studies that show people are **three times** more likely to put something away if the home is clearly labeled.

- Bulletin boards work really well to help you organize your schedules, to-do lists, and even your thoughts in a clearly visible manner! You really need to take advantage of your vertical wall space more than any other bug! Chalkboard walls, white boards, corkboards and other display boards are key to keeping your home running smoothly.

- Butterflies are easily distracted by their own clutter. Have a friend or family member help you with your bigger organizing projects in order to keep you on track. Invite someone over and ask him or her to help you sort your items and choose things to

be donated or tossed out. Once the piles are sorted and paired down, you and your helper can place your items into colorful or clear baskets and put them away.

- Use the four-sort method when organizing any space. Have four labeled or color coded baskets, bags, or boxes handy: one for **Trash**, one for **Donate**, one for **Does Not Belong in This Area**, and one for **Keep**. This will help you stay focused and make purging, sorting, and donating your items easier. Butterflies can become distracted if they are moving from room to room to put items away. Wait until one room or space is done before putting away the DOES NOT BELONG items.

- Have a clear vision for your space. Take a before picture of the mess right now and then find a picture in a magazine or online of what you want your space to look like when you are done. Hang both of these in your room somewhere for a visual reminder and motivation. **Butterflies are visually motivated and this trick can really help you stay on track.**

- A 21 **Item Toss** every month is a great way for Butterflies to purge. Butterflies and Bees really need to make purging a priority in order to have a space they can easily maintain. Remind yourself that **less is more** and that by removing the items you don't love, use, or find beautiful, you will be able to see the things you do love much more easily. Find out more about this painless purging trick in the next chapter.

- Schedule organizing time each and every day. Schedule in fifteen minutes each day and work on one small part of your space. Try to pick the same time every day, like right after the kids go to bed each night. The average one hour television show has fifteen minutes of commercials, so you can easily squeeze in some quick organizing time while you watch your favorite show!

- Hooks are a Butterfly's best friend! Hang hooks in your entrance way, inside your closet, and on the back of all of your doors! A hook is the best way to ensure you will hang up your coat, bag, and everything else you tend to struggle putting away!

- Open-shelving works best for you! Take advantage of vertical space and get stuff off your floor. Invest in shelving and closet organizers in order to maximize your storage. While I always say that organization should never be expensive, investing in shelving is always worth it! Your shelving doesn't have to be expensive, though, and you can find amazing storage solutions at thrift stores, garage sales, and online swap sales. My favorite place to buy shelving units is always Ikea.

- Remember, stuff is just stuff. Don't put your belongings above your family or yourself. Clutter can have a very negative impact on children and relationships, and just by getting rid of the things you do not use or love, you can drastically improve the quality of life for your entire family.

- Practice the "One Minute Rule." Butterflies tend to procrastinate cleaning and putting things away when they are done with them. Remind yourself often that if something takes "One Minute or Less" to accomplish, do it right now! "Later" should be a word that you work hard to erase for your vocabulary.

CRICKET

A Cricket is a classic piler! They are very neat and tidy piles, but piles nonetheless. Crickets tend to be very logical and practical, and like things organized in a very certain way. Once a filing or organizing system is set in place, a Cricket will have no problem following it…it's just a matter of finding the time to setup that right system!

Crickets are often quite organized and maybe even a bit over organized. Crickets like very detailed and logical organizing systems, which can sometimes take too much time to setup or require too much effort to use properly. Therefore, Crickets will stack neat piles until they have time to put them away properly or until they have "dealt with" and finished using the item completely.

Most Crickets are perfectionists. They feel that if they can't do something perfectly, why bother doing it at all. This can lead to a build-up of multiple to-do piles that can easily get out of control.

The best solution for a Cricket is to let go a little bit. Crickets need to remind themselves that creating "good enough" organizing systems for their items today is better than creating perfect homes for their items tomorrow. You can always go back and fine-tune an organizing system when you have the time to spare, but in the meantime, at least it is neat and organized and not taking up valuable surface space in your home.

Try "macro-organizing" your piles instead of "micro-organizing" them. Here is an example: Joe wants to file his financial paperwork into a filing system. He wants a filing system for all of his investments, with separate, labeled folders for each year and each different account. He also wants separate folders for each bank account and one for each of his children's college funds. In the meantime, all his papers are stacked in neat piles on his desk and have been for months. A good solution would be to make one file called "Investments" and file everything together for the meantime. He can always "micro-organize" this file folder at a later time, but at least it is put away today! Here are some good organizing solutions for Crickets:

- Set up a vertical filing system, like a magazine rack, close to your desk or a wherever you tend to pile your important papers. This will be your "Action File." Place important papers you need to deal with here, in sorted and labeled slots. Remember, horizontal is hidden and vertical is visible. Papers that are piled can easily become forgotten about and invisible to you, while papers stored vertically are easily seen and will be a visual reminder.

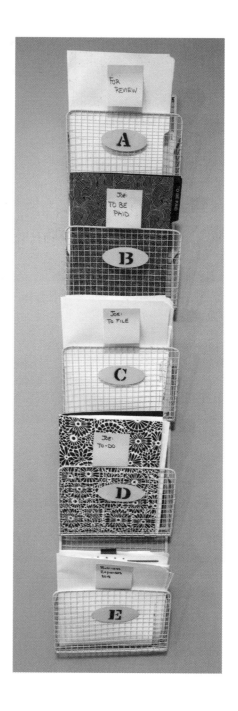

- Set a timer when organizing to encourage you to move fast and stay focused. Crickets are very task-oriented, and a timer can be a very efficient motivating tool.

- Invest in a scanner, or at the very least a filing cabinet. Crickets can really benefit from going paperless, since paper is usually the biggest organizing issue they struggle with. Some Crickets find it easier to file all of their papers electronically.

- Invest in a label maker. If you do have to file papers, using a label maker can not only make setting up filing systems faster, but it can also help make the systems even more efficient and easy to use.

- Place open baskets or bins on your desk, kitchen counter, or other surface to hold your piles until you can get to them. A full basket will be a visual reminder that your stack is getting too big for the basket and it is time to put it away.

- Make yourself a to-do list on a traditional pad of paper, on your phone, or in your calendar. Crickets, more than any other bug, can really benefit from daily, weekly, and monthly to-do lists, as they are motivated to check items off their physical list.

The motivation to complete lists can make crickets very high-achievers.

- Turn off distractions, like your phone, email, and television when starting an organizing project. Crickets work best while listening to music or audiobooks while they work. Remind yourself that creating efficient organizing systems will save you time and effort in the long run and should be a priority to you.

- Paper is kryptonite to your organizational super powers. Invest in a paper shredder and use it—often!

- Remind yourself that **perfectionism leads to procrastination**. Sometimes good enough for now is really…good enough. This will be hard for Crickets at first, but with practice, you will start to see that you can accomplish so much more when you let go of the need to make everything perfect all the time. Organizing something "good enough" today is always better than putting it off until the "perfect time." You can always go back and tweak and improve on your systems at a later date.

LADYBUG

Ladybugs are enigmas! Have you ever seen a real ladybug (like, the actual bug) with their wings open? Yuck. With their wings closed, they are adorable with beautifully bright red and shiny polka dotted shells, but once those wings open up, it is a freaking horror show under there! That is basically exactly the same as a "Ladybug's" home. The main living areas tend to be tidy and even beautifully decorated, but under the surface, they are shoving and hiding like the "hidey-hoarders" they really are!

Ladybugs are generally stressed out by surface clutter and strive to keep their living space clean and clutter-free. You know you're a Ladybug if your surfaces are clean and tidy, but your junk drawer is overflowing and you may be impaled by falling junk when you open your closet. Without a mirco-organizing system in place, the small stuff can get shoved here, there, and everywhere! Ladybugs need to work on setting up systems inside drawers and closets that are quick and easy to use. Here are some tips just for the Ladybug:

- Set aside fifteen minutes per week (or even more often) and pick one "hidden" area in your home to reorganize. Ladybugs can easily follow most organizing systems; they just need to schedule time to make it a priority.

- Use drawer dividers or small open containers to keep like items together inside **each and every one of your drawers.** Examples: batteries, pens, tools, jewellery, makeup, tape, craft supplies, etc. Using dividers or open containers means you can just open the drawer and easily toss the item in its home! Drawer dividers are a MUST for Ladybugs in order to keep those spaces tidy and organized.

- **If it is hard to put away, you won't do it.** Make sure your storage solutions are easily accessible and clearly labeled. Use containers without lids inside drawers, closets, and just about everywhere else! Open-lidded containers allow you to still toss and hide your items in your hidden areas, but in an organized and easy-to-find later way. If you have to stop and take the lid off your storage container, you are likely to just set the item on top.

- Invest in baskets that you find beautiful. Baskets are your best friend! Ladybugs love a pretty, clutter-free home. Using attractive baskets can keep your home looking gorgeous and uncluttered while giving you an easy-to-access spot to store smaller items. Use baskets for toys, newspapers, cookbooks, office supplies, and so much more!

- Binder systems will work well for you! Using a binder with clear plastic sleeves is a great way to hold your important family papers, like schedules, calendars, contact numbers, recipes, coupons, school information, and kids' artwork. Binders keep your important papers out of sight, but they are still organized and easy to access.

- Create "zones" in every room in your home. Take a look at how each room is currently functioning, and create "homes" for all of your stuff based on the area in that room where you use it. Do your children do their homework and crafts at the kitchen table? Make sure your homework and craft supplies are located in the kitchen, somewhere close to the table! Organizing into zones will ensure that cleaning up is fast and easy.

Ladybugs can easily get caught up in their homes. Be sure to take time out of your day for family and friends. There is more to life than a clean and organized home...wait, did I just say that?

BEE

A Bee is someone who always has a new project or hobby on the go! Busy Bees tend to work hard and play harder. They almost always like to keep their tools, papers, and supplies out in plain sight until they have finished the job or hobby they are working on. This can quickly turn into a big clutter problem, as Bees are known for having many projects or hobbies going on at the same time.

There are lots of different kinds of Bees. Some have work projects, which come with mounds of paperwork to deal with, and others have many different hobbies and activities they enjoy, which require mountains of supplies and tools. Some Bees have home-based businesses that can overrun the entire household with materials necessary for their business (and some do not). Reading is also a hobby, and if a Bee is an avid reader, chances are he is drowning in books, magazines, or newspapers.

A love for cooking and baking is a hobby that can come with a lot of clutter. A Bee who loves to create in the kitchen tends to have every tool he could ever possibly need and never enough storage room for it all. A culinary-loving Bee's kitchen usually has little to no counter space available because it is filled with all of his kitchen gadgets and supplies.

Bees almost always come with a lot of stuff. Whether it be exercise equipment, scrapbooking supplies, photographs, art supplies, books, cooking and baking utensils, wood working materials, home improvement tools, or any other supplies used during a hobby, it can quickly take over your space.

Some suggestions for a Busy Bee? First, try to have no more than three projects on the go at once. If you have had an unfinished project for a long time, it may be time to get rid of it all together and open yourself (and your space) up to new projects you are more passionate about. Do you have a lot of exercise equipment that hasn't been used in years? As hard as it is, perhaps it is time to donate or sell that equipment and use the space for another hobby you would actually enjoy, like a reading room or scrapbooking space. Do you really need that many pots and pans, screwdrivers, stickers, or books? The answer is almost always no.

Bees are the masters of good intentions, but there are only so many hours in a day and only so much we can reasonably get done. **There also comes a point when we need to admit that even though something may be useful, it is taking away space that could be used for more important items.** Here are some tips just for Bees:

- Make a priority list for yourself and your home. Is having a clean kitchen a priority over finishing your scrapbook? Then make time for what is a priority for you and finish **that task before you start a new one.**

- Learn to let go. Bees tend to keep things just in case they may need them someday. If you don't love it and you haven't used it in a year, get rid of it. While this is hard for most Bees to do, remind yourself that if you have not used something in over a year, the odds are that you never will. Freeing up more space can make working on the things you love even more enjoyable.

- Schedule, schedule, schedule. Your time is precious to you, so make the most of it. Make sure you have a monthly calendar you can reference easily, and create daily schedules and daily and weekly chore lists. Busy Bees can benefit more than any other bug from a well-planned daily schedule.

- Make a list of all the things you want to do that day (make it reasonable!), and work on those things (and only those things). If you can't get them all done, carry the left over items to the next day's list.

- Purge, purge, purge. Do you really need that many screwdrivers? Do you really use all of those rubber stamps? How many different kitchen gadgets do you really use on a regular basis? Bees collect things for their projects and often end up with too many unused materials.

- Use project boxes. Have a box or basket with **all the supplies you need** for your current project (stackable banker boxes work great for Bees). When you are done for the day, put the items back into the box until you can work on it again. This way your supplies are out of the way, but you don't need to take everything out again to work on your project next time. Be sure to clearly label your project box! This will help keep the areas of your home you share with your family free from your clutter.

In every family there are usually several different types of ClutterBugs all living together in one house. Because of these very different organizing styles, it can be difficult to put systems in place that work for everyone. Having an opposite organizing style than a spouse or loved one can cause stress, tension, and resentment. If you are a Ladybug who needs a clean and clutter-free space, living with a Butterfly who needs to visualize her items can be frustrating.

By identifying and understanding your family members' unique styles, you can work together to create organizing solutions that work for everyone. Colorful, clearly labeled bins on a cube-shelving unit is the perfect compromise for both Ladybugs and Butterflies who share a living space. Butterflies can easily see the labels and know where everything they need is stored, but Ladybugs do not have to see the various items stored inside.

Just the realization that everyone organizes differently and learning a few tips and tricks for each bug can greatly reduce stress and solve most of your clutter issues.

Now that you have discovered your personal organizing style, let's roll up our sleeves and jump-start your journey to a clean and clutter-free home!

TIME
Spent with family

Is worth every

SECOND

Just 15 Minutes a Day Keeps the Clutter Away

Now that you know what ClutterBug you are, hopefully you can better understand why you organize your home the way you do, or why it looks like an absolute disaster zone (sorry Butterflies, I'm talking about you). No matter what bug you are, when it comes to organizing our homes, the process in the beginning is the same for everyone. The way our styles differ is in the type of systems that keep us organized. Butterflies and Bees need colorful or clear baskets that are really visible and easy to access, while Ladybugs and Crickets prefer more hidden, out-of-sight storage options. The process we take to actually get organized is exactly the same, right up until we purchase or create our storage solutions.

Unfortunately, purchasing bins and baskets is the final part of organization. Most people purchase bins, baskets, and other storage containers first, hoping some new tote or shelving unit is going to magically solve their clutter issues. I hate to break it to you, but putting your stuff in a plastic container is not going to make your room look like a page from House and Home magazine. **I think trying to buy our way out of a messy house with different organizing products is the biggest reason why so many of us have failed at actually getting and staying organized.** We buy plastic bins to throw at our clutter, hoping it will make us organized, and we end up with stacked bins shoved full of random junk everywhere. Often times, we forget about the junk we have stored away, and end up having to buy and replace stuff we already own because we have no idea where it is. This vicious cycle of buying plastic containers to hide away our stuff just creates even more clutter. Let's stop the madness!

Almost every client I have ever worked with has had an unhealthy amount of plastic storage containers. Large Rubbermaid totes, those plastic three-drawer-on-wheels atrocities (that rarely work for anyone), and endless plastic containers in all shapes and sizes. Many of my clients had towering stacks of empty containers they bought, only to discover they did not work for their needs. These misused containers almost always get banished to the basement to die. In many cases, the storage solutions they bought to contain the clutter was literally creating more clutter than the original clutter (let's play a game and count how often I say "clutter" in this book)!

Can we just all agree to never buy one of those three drawer plastic storage containers again? In fact, let's all make signs and protest outside of Walmart, shouting, "Hey ho, those containers got to go!" It isn't just that they are really ugly; they never work and I want to start boycotting them. Whenever I see someone attempting to use them to organize, I need to contain my rage (if you use them and they work for you, please don't send me hate mail…you are a special exception).

So, if you are not supposed to start with buying storage solutions, then where do you start?

To get really organized and **stay that way for good**, you need to first identify the most troubled areas in your home and make a plan. **An organizing plan for your home is like a road map to clutter free success.**

Before we can be really successful in reaching our goals, we have to define what those goals are. Writing down a list of exactly how you want your home to look and function is a crucial step towards making your goals a reality.

Writing down goals properly requires you to think of your main goal and then work backwards to develop a plan to get there. One of my life goals is to be ridiculously wealthy. Just a blanket statement goal such as that is hard to achieve; you need to develop a plan on how to achieve that goal, like stepping stones to success. I've yet to work out all the details of my ridiculously-wealthy life goal, but I'm pretty sure "write super awesome organizing book" is one of the first steps!

Fortunately for you, if your goal is to have an organized and beautiful home, it will be much easier for you to develop your plan to get there!

ClutterBug.Me
What clutterbug are you?
Visit clutterbug.me for more great printables.

ORGANIZATION PLANNER
Your Plan of Attack

ORGANIZING PROJECT:

WHAT ISN'T WORKING?

15 MINUTE ORGANIZING TO DO'S:

- ○
- ○
- ○
- ○
- ○
- ○
- ○
- ○

SCHEDULE IT!

S	M	T	W	T	F	S

Visit clutterbug.me for more great printables.

ClutterBug.Me
What clutterbug are you?
Visit clutterbug.me for more great printables.

ORGANIZATION PLANNER
Your Plan of Attack

ORGANIZING PROJECT: **Master Bedroom**

WHAT ISN'T WORKING?

Clutter on dresser
Too many clothes in closet
Dresser drawers are too full
Chair always has laundry on it
Not enough hangers
Not enough storage space

15 MINUTE ORGANIZING TO DO'S:

○ Place "catch all" basket on top of dresser
○ Purge 21 items from dresser drawers
○ Purge of all holey and unpaired socks
○ Neatly fold all t-shirts
○ Install extra hanging rod in closet
○ Purge 21 items from closet
○ Install hooks behind the door for "not that dirty" clothing
○

SCHEDULE IT!

S	M	T	W	T	F	S
Organize Dresser	Install rod and hooks	Purge socks	Fold t-shirts	Purge closet	Buy Basket	Enjoy Clean Room!

Start by creating an Organizing Road Map for each and every room in your home. Here is an example of an organizing road map for my bedroom.

When filling out your Organizing Plan, choose the areas that have the **biggest clutter issues** first. Are you frustrated by your cluttered kitchen counters? Does your master bedroom make you want to run screaming from the room instead of wanting to stay and relax?

By choosing the areas of your home that will have the biggest day-to-day impact on your life first, you will feel energized and motivated to keep going!

The trick to creating a successful organizing plan is to break your organizing projects down into manageable, fifteen minute projects. This is the key to staying motivated and to creating a lifelong organizing routine.

15 minutes a day can keep the clutter away!

You may think that fifteen minutes does not sound like a lot of time, but let me assure you that you can accomplish a lot in that amount of time!

It takes less than fifteen minutes to reorganize a junk drawer, and let me tell you: organizing your junk drawer will change your life. You probably think I'm overreaching here, but I promise you, it will absolutely change your life. Before I got organized, I could never find the scissors. It's a small thing, but I would have to look around and search through messy drawers to find a pair almost every single day. Now that I organized my junk drawer properly, I save time each and every time I use it. Just saving me one minute a day looking for scissors will save me 30,000 minutes over the course of my lifetime. That is over 500 hours and over twenty total days! **Yep, looking for something for just one minute a day is stealing more than twenty days of your precious life!** So yeah, organizing your junk drawer really will change your life.

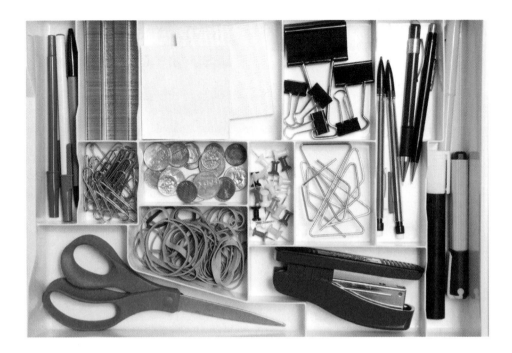

Choose just one cupboard in your kitchen a day to make more efficient and functional instead of trying to do the entire kitchen at once. If your closet is a mess, choose just one rod of clothing to go through at a time, instead of every article of clothing that you own.

Of course you can tackle more if you want to, but by breaking your projects down into manageable chunks of time, you will never get overwhelmed and left with unfinished organizing projects, which can make you feel like a failure. **The secret to staying motivated is that wonderful feeling of accomplishment and pride that comes with starting and completing an organized space!** I am totally an organizing junkie now. I literally get a little "high" from organizing my sock drawer...I may need to get some sort of a life outside my home!

I, like millions of other people, recently read a widely successful organizing book that encouraged people to grab everything in one category and pile it in the middle of a room. You are then supposed to go through that pile and only keep the items that bring you "joy". While I loved the concept of this book— and it has seemed to work for so many people—I found it to be an unrealistic approach for me. I am busy… and kind of lazy. I have three kids, pets, and way too much junk. I don't have time to pull out every single item of clothing in our home and pile it in the living room. And after pulling all that stuff out, I most certainly would have zero desire, or time, to put it all away neatly again. I must admit, when I read that book I was kind of like, are you for real??? That type of organizing approach, while it may be effective, takes hours and hours to complete each project. Who has time for that?

For me, I need the fifteen minute a day approach. It is a realistic and easily managed amount of time to dedicate to organizing your home each day. Maybe I have ADD, but I become completely bored half way through big projects and usually end up abandoning them to go and watch Netflix. I need quick and easy projects I can completely finish before my ADD brain kicks in and forces me to move on. You should see me try and paint a room, it never ends well. **The average one hour television show has more than fifteen minutes of commercials, which puts the amount of time you will spend to get a clean and clutter-free home in perspective.**

Even the most cluttered and dysfunctional homes can be transformed this way, I promise. This method works amazingly well for a number of reasons. First, everyone can find time for just fifteen minutes a day, no matter how busy his or her schedule (or how lazy we feel that day). Secondly, having quick and easy projects means we can actually complete the task we start, giving us a sense of pride and accomplishment and keep the motivation going. Lastly, once you have worked this method into your daily schedule for a few weeks, it will become a second nature habit that you no longer have to force yourself to do.

Let's be real for a minute. If you, like me, struggle with clutter and housework, we have probably developed some bad habits along the way that have put us in this situation. Being messy is a habit, and habits are hard to change overnight.

The good news is you can develop new habits and it only takes about thirty days to make it happen. If you spend just 15 minutes a day organizing your home, not only will it look a million times better at the end of just one month, but you will now have made daily organizing a life-long habit!

So while I love the concept of that highly successful organizing book (which was self-titled as being "life-changing" and "magic"), the truth is, **even if we got rid of every unused and unloved thing in our homes today, our homes would just fill up again before we knew it.** We are constantly acquiring new things, whether we like it or not. Children outgrow clothing, we receive gifts throughout the year, and there are always little things here and there coming into our homes each and every month. **Unless we learn to deal with clutter and organize our belongings a little bit everyday, our homes would just fill up again overtime and we would be forced to continue repeating the process over and over again.**

This is how I transformed my home in just fifteen minutes a day:

When my daughter Abby was born, my first daughter Izzy wasn't even two years old. I wanted to have my kids close together so that they could be lifelong best friends (fingers crossed it works out) but I had no idea how much freaking work two under two would actually be. I suddenly found myself a stay-at-home mom with a toddler and a baby and needless to say, housework was not a priority. Getting through the day with all three of us fed and somewhat clean was basically my only priority.

I remember feeling like I was working all day long, but I was literally accomplishing nothing. I did, however, spend hours every day just looking for stuff I had misplaced, like my car keys. Oh my word, those freaking car keys. I would constantly lose them or my wallet or my cell phone...and sometimes the baby (well, just that one time). I felt like a giant failure as a mother and as a homemaker.

By the time Abby was nine months old, I had started a home daycare and well, you can imagine how my house looked after that. My days were pretty much filled with snot, poop, and singing the same brain-numbing kid songs a thousand times. I was exhausted, overwhelmed, and had zero time for myself.

So what changed? What was the trigger that transformed my home and my life from chaos and clutter to calm and clean? Peter Walsh. I discovered a show on TLC called Clean Sweep and it literally changed my life. The entire television show was dedicated to transforming families and their homes through organization. After watching a few episodes and absorbing every word Peter said, I bought all of his books and began my new life as a crazy, obsessed-with-all-things-organizing person.

I'll never forget the first time I organized something and it stayed organized (for longer than a nanosecond)! **It was my master bedroom closet and I used the same method that almost every Professional Organizer uses when organizing a client's home. I used the SPACE acronym.** This method works and (thankfully for me), it makes organizing fast and easy (even for us ADD moms).

S is for SORT

P is for PURGE

A is for ASSIGN

C is for CONTAIN

E is for EVALUATE

I started by taking everything that was in my side of the closet out. Then, following the SPACE method, I started with "S" for Sort. I sorted all of my clothing into similar piles. Long sleeve shirts together, short sleeve, skirts, pants… you get the idea!

Then came the "P" part of the process… the dreaded Purge part. I went through each sorted pile and picked out the items I didn't like and the ones that did not fit.

I heard Peter's gorgeous Australian accent in my head telling me to remember the 80/20 rule. **The truth is, we wear only 20 percent of our wardrobe, 80 percent of the time.** This tidbit of knowledge made getting rid of those ugly shirts much easier. Yes, I spent $50 on that hideous sweater, but it was still hideous and therefore not worth keeping. It was easy to let it go when I reminded myself I was making room for the clothing I loved and wore often.

Sorting into piles makes purging much faster and easier. With a heaping pile of sixteen pairs of black pants, it was suddenly obvious I had way too many and could easily purge my least favorites. I will share so many more painless purging methods with you in Chapter Three.

Next came the "A" for Assign. We are going to talk more about this important step in the next few chapters. For my closet, I assigned my pants and skirts to the bottom rod and my shirts on the top rod, which was easier to see and access. I usually wore the same pair of pants a few times, but I always wore a new shirt everyday. Because I wore a new shirt more often than new pants, I assigned them the easiest to access area in my closet. We will discuss why this step is so important in getting and staying organized in Chapter Four.

Now came my favorite part of the organizing process, "C" for Contain! I took a look at the piles I had left after hanging all of my pants and tops, and found that I had a small pile for workout clothing (evidence of my hatred for sweating), one for bathing suits, and a large pile of pyjamas (pyjama pants are totally acceptable to wear to Walmart, right?). Now that I could easily see each pile of clothing already sorted, I could see exactly what size container I needed for each sorted pile. Our bedroom was small and had no space for a dresser, so our tiny closet had to accommodate almost every article of clothing I owned. I purchased some containers from my local dollar store for each of the remaining piles, labeled those containers and put them on the bottom shelves in my closet. Voilà! An organized and functional closet!

The final "E" in the SPACE method is for Evaluate. As you acquire new belongings, or as you and your family use the space, you may need to re-evaluate and tweak your organizing system until you get it right. Understanding and working with systems for your unique organizing style will be a big part of this step.

This first project took me about thirty minutes to complete, which was longer than the fifteen minutes a day I recommend, but still a reasonable amount of time to complete and see immediate results!

When I was done with my closet, the final result was an organized and functional space that actually stayed clean and organized. The real impact came the next morning, when I woke up late and had to rush to get dressed before my daycare children arrived. I was able to find my clothing so easily and in **half the time it usually took.** Here is where the life-changing magic stuff gets real! Those thirty minutes I invested in reorganizing my closet continued to save me time every morning when I got dressed. **It was at that moment I realized that creating an organizing system was an investment of my time—an investment that would continue to pay for years and years to come.**

After I completed my closet, I was so amazed at how much more functional it was that I starting picking one small organizing project to do every day in my home. One day it was my sock drawer, the next day just one cupboard in my kitchen. Before I knew it I was looking forward to my daily organizing time, and my home was transforming into a clutter-free oasis right before my eyes.

Now, six years later, I still spend fifteen minutes a day on my home. Some days it is simply tidying up our main living areas, and other days it is reorganizing or straightening a drawer or cupboard. Once a week I spend fifteen minutes doing a **21 Item Toss** (I cover this painless technique in the next chapter) just to be sure that my home never becomes a cluttered TLC-special kind of house again.

If you take nothing else from this book, just please remember, transforming your home doesn't have to be an overwhelming or expensive undertaking. All it takes is just fifteen minutes and the willingness to start, right now.

CHAPTER THREE

Painless Purging

So, what is clutter anyway? I define clutter as two things. **First, it is any object that is not put away in its proper home.** This is the clutter that is found on flat surfaces like counters, the top of your dresser, and sometimes even piled on the floor. This type of clutter is basically an overflow of everyday life, or "lazy clutter" (because we were too darn lazy to put it away). The second type of clutter is the overabundance of stuff. This type of clutter is the fifty picture frames on every wall throughout your home, the collection of ceramic bears on every furniture surface or the one hundred books on the shelf you have already read and never will again.

We live in a world of "buy now, pay later," where we are constantly bombarded by ads promising us that acquiring some new gadget or thing-a-majiggy is going to make us happier, healthier,

and improve the quality of our life. What we actually end up with is so much stuff that those piles of empty promises make us sad, sick, and desperate for a change. I've been there, done that and I am literally writing the book about it. "Stuff" doesn't make us happy, but having a clutter-free home certainly can!

I would love to tell you it's possible to have a beautiful and organized home without getting rid of anything, but that would be a dirty, rotten lie. **Purging is probably the most important step in getting organized and the most difficult step of the process.**

Just in case you are planning on skimming this chapter, let me start with my most important tidbit of advice first: **don't overthink it. Trust your first instinct.** When deciding whether to keep something or to donate it, make the choice fast and stick with your first decision. You are not trying to decide which child to keep, it's just stuff. Second guessing yourself is just going to make the process much more difficult. **Remember, your belongings are replaceable, but your time and well-being are not.**

I'm going to start this chapter with a quick story about one of my most challenging clients who had an extremely difficult time letting things go. Let's call her Susie. Susie was a school teacher, lived in a beautiful home, and had a loving family. She hired me to help organize her home office, and when I first entered her house, I was excited by what I saw. Everything was neat and clutter-free and Susie seemed to have it all together. This is going to be a piece of cake, I thought. When she opened the door to her office, though, my optimism sagged: it was full, waist-high full, with every square inch of floor space covered with huge piles of junk.

I've dealt with this level of clutter before. The difficult part was that Susie wanted to keep all of it, and have it all fit in her tiny office space (while looking beautiful, spacious, and clutter-free, of course). When I asked for her vision for the room, she told me she wanted an "open and airy oasis to do yoga and meditate." Her vision for the room could not be further from reality, and there was no

way we could make it happen without some serious purging. Susie assumed I had some tricks that could just organize everything, transforming her office into a clean and minimalist space. I'm a Professional Organizer, not a magician. Even with the addition of a bazillion shelving units and every basket on earth, she just had way too much stuff to ever fit properly in such a small room.

Trying to get her to purge was a nightmare. Everything was important or special to her, despite it being buried under three feet of clutter, and despite the fact that she hadn't even stepped foot inside her office in over three years. Susie agonized over every single piece of paper. Filling a small shopping bag of clutter to donate took weeks instead of the minutes it should have. I had originally scheduled and quoted forty hours (which I thought would be more than enough time) with Susie to reorganize her office. **Three months later**, I was still dragging myself to her home each week in hope that she would finally see the light.

So what happened? I got real with her. To tell the truth, I lost my temper and unclenched my tongue, and let everything I was thinking finally fall out of my face in one epic and unprofessional monologue.

It went something like this:

"Susie. You are killing me. I feel like I'm dying right here and now on the floor of your office. All of this stuff is just junk. You hate coming into this office, it makes you stressed and overwhelmed and you probably forgot half of this crap was even in here. You want your own private space to make you feel calm and relaxed, don't you? **You are more important than anything in here.** You need this space. You deserve this relaxing oasis. **Nothing in here is more important than your happiness.** This crap has got to go, like today."

While I wasn't proud of my inappropriate outburst, it was exactly what she needed to hear. Susie needed tough love. She was letting her useless junk control her life, and it was taking away from her the things she really wanted most. That was the breakthrough we needed to finally purge over 75 percent of the clutter she had piled in that room.

I still keep in contact with Susie to this day. She loves her little yoga studio and she doesn't miss or regret **one single thing** she got rid of. Don't be the old Susie. **Don't get so hung up on your "stuff" that you lose sight of what you really want from your home.**

Here is the harsh reality of our precious "stuff:" the more we have, the more it takes from us. It takes our time to clean and maintain it, it takes our money to buy and store it, and it takes a toll on us emotionally when it begins to pile up.

When your home is cluttered and out of control, you can't help but feel out of control yourself. It is impossible to feel calm and relaxed when you are frantically searching for your keys, or stressed because you've forgotten to pay a bill... again. When you wake up in the morning and the first thing you see is a messy bedroom with piles of laundry and chores waiting for you, it is hard to feel energized and positive about your day.

Let's make a commitment to each other right here and right now. **Let's agree that we are not going to let our "stuff" control our lives and steal our time any longer.**

Invisible Clutter

Before I really get going with the down and dirty stuff, I feel like telling you another story.

My grandma used to collect bears. She started collecting little ceramic bears years ago and that collection grew and grew. At every holiday and birthday, people would buy my grandmother more freaking bears. Stuffed bears, bear artwork, bear figurines, bear dishes and even a teddy bear toilet seat cover. Trust me, I could not make this stuff up. At one point, I kid you not, **every single surface was filled with teddy bears.** The first time I brought my now-husband to her house for a visit, his eyes literally bugged out of his head. We had to sit on top of stuffed bears that were piled on the sofa while drinking tea from teddy bear teacups. Her house was always clean, but the bear thing was like a TLC special.

A few years ago, my Grandma had knee surgery and had to live in an assisted living apartment for a couple of months while she recovered. This minimal and clutter-free apartment helped her to make a startling revelation. **She didn't** even like teddy bears anymore. She hadn't even realized how cluttered and full her home was until she moved back in after her recovery. **Those thousands of bears had become invisible to her.** Despite feeling guilty about getting rid of all of the gifts she had received over the years, my Grandma packed up and donated almost every single one of those bears. She now loves her beautiful and clutter-free home more than ever, and I'm no longer creeped out when I go to visit (sorry, Grandma).

Sometimes we get caught up in the fun of acquiring, and let's be honest, buying new things feels good. Unfortunately, taking care of these things usually does not; no one wants to dust 999 ceramic bears every week.

Take a minute to survey your home. Really look at it. The thing about clutter is, overtime, it becomes invisible to us. After seeing it day after day, we just become numb to it and we stop noticing it all together. Unfortunately, it is only invisible to us; any guests that come over to visit can see our piles of junk just fine! The same things can be said for smells. People who stink rarely know that they stink. It is like they have become immune to their own smell. Clutter has the same effect. You may have a smelly, cluttered home and not even know it!

So how can we finally see our invisible clutter? Easy, we take a picture! Have you ever had your picture taken and looked at it later and thought, who in the heck is that? There is no way I actually look like that! That, my friend, is the story of my life. I ride the denial train on a daily basis. Whenever I see a picture of myself, I'm always left in a state of absolute shock (in my mind, I'm a total babe) and I had the same reaction the first time I took photos of my home.

When I started YouTubing and blogging, I began taking pictures of my space to upload for the world to see. I wanted to share my organizing journey and my progress along the way. Unfortunately, unlike a selfie, I couldn't blur out my home's imperfections before uploading the pictures to the Internet. There is no "remove the random garbage everywhere" filter on Instagram. Taking a photo forced me to see the clutter that had been completely invisible to me before. And boy, did I have clutter. Why did I have so many half-empty glasses of water all over my side table? Maybe it was a subconscious thing after watching the movie Signs too many times, but honestly, I hadn't really noticed them there before. By taking photos, I was able to really see my space from an outside perspective, and it was totally an eye-opening experience.

Purging Tips and Tricks

The one question I get asked over and over again, more than any other question, is:

> "I want to get organized, but where do I start?"

The best place to start is with purging! You will see a huge impact immediately just by removing a few things from your home.

Now I have gotten to the point where I actually love filling a garbage bag with my unused belongings to donate to charity. Purging my home makes me feel so great that I'm always a little shocked when I have to start the process from the beginning with a new client. At first, before regular purging becomes a fun part of your routine, it can actually seem a little sucky.

No worries though, I have learned some great techniques that can help make purging easy and fun. I have spent months, years even, trying to convince my clients to let go of their unused belongings. Some methods worked better than others, and some clients caused me to age ten years during the process. In the end, it was those epic battles that taught me the best ways to purge clutter.

Here are a few of my **favorite purging tips** that will make getting rid of clutter absolutely painless.

Garbage Bag Therapy

This is an easy and effective way to make a dent in your home's clutter, without having to make any hard decisions about what to keep and what not to. Grab a garbage bag (and a bag for recycling) and start searching your home for just that, garbage. I like to call this "Garbage Bag Therapy" because it is actually very therapeutic. You are going to feel energized and have that wonderful rush of accomplishment and pride that comes with de-cluttering, without having the anxiety that people can feel when letting go of their belongings. **You will be shocked at how much actual garbage you can find in your home, even if it looks pretty clean and clutter-free!** Old receipts stuffed in drawers, expired medications and cosmetics, empty shampoo bottles in the shower, packaging from purchases that will never be returned, empty envelopes and junk mail are just a few pieces of garbage that most homes have lying around. Open drawers and closets and search your flat surfaces finding as much trash as you can to get out of your home today.

I love starting with this purging method as a warm-up because it has all the highs and feel good stuff that comes from purging without any of the stress that comes with making those tough decisions. It truly is "painless purging," and is the perfect way to jump-start your journey to a clean and clutter-free home. So grab a garbage bag and do the trash-tango today!

21 Item Toss

My favorite method for reducing clutter and staying clutter-free long term is to do a "21 Item Toss" on a regular basis. I have no idea why, but having a set number of items you need to find and donate (or recycle) is so much more motivating than trying to purge without a goal. I have found that twenty-one is the perfect number, the purging sweet spot if you will! It isn't so high that it's overwhelming, but it's a high enough number that it will push you to find a few extra things to reach the total of twenty-one.

I do a 21 Item Toss all the time, still to this day! Most of the time I can easily get to eighteen or nineteen things, and I have to push myself to make it all the way to twenty-one. Sometimes I get carried away and grab shirts and pants from my husband's side of the closet, just so I can make it to twenty-one. He has never even noticed, so obviously nothing of his that I purged with this method was that important. I have also been known to make my three-year-old toss in a toy

or two so Mommy can hit her twenty-one item goal! I know; I'm an awful person.

In your master bedroom, find twenty-one articles of clothing that you can donate. This is way easier to do than you think, and it can take just a few minutes to accomplish. Pick nine to ten shirts that you never wear, three to four pairs of paints or skirts, two to three sets of pyjamas, one bathing suit, four pairs of underwear that have seen better days, and toss in a few pairs of holey socks! Add in that tie you find hideous or that scarf you never wear and you are already over your total! Easy and painless. You can choose whatever you want to toss into your donation bag (or recycle bag), and take just a few short minutes to find twenty-one items around your home.

If your home is very cluttered, you may need to do this every day until you get your home to a point where you can switch over to maintenance mode. For my home, I schedule a 21 Item Toss each and every month. I can always find garbage, old papers and magazines, and even a few items that I no longer need (or I find some of my family's things). This method was critical for me in the beginning when an overwhelming mess surrounded us, and I still use it today to keep clutter at bay.

The 4 Sort Method

This purging method is really visual and hands-on, so it is perfect for both Butterflies and Bees when it comes to de-cluttering any space. I find this method works best in very cluttered or large spaces, and it makes it easy to sort and purge a huge amount of stuff in very little time.

Start with four boxes, bags or anything else that can be used to sort your belongings. This is made easier if whatever you are using to sort can be easily carried once full and if you can toss things into it without much effort. Personally, I like using plastic or mesh laundry baskets for this job!

Make four large labels for each basket, bag, or box. You will need one label that says DONATE, one for TRASH, one for KEEP, and one for DOES NOT BELONG. If you are a Butterfly, it can help to use different colors for each labels! Attach the labels to your sorting bins and place the bins in the middle of the room you are tackling.

This method works the same way, whether you're de-cluttering a drawer, closet or an entire room! If you are doing an entire room, I recommend breaking the room into sections and just doing one section at a time, i.e. toys, books, craft supplies, etc. Now, just start sorting! **Pick up items and make decisions as fast as you can about whether you want to keep it, donate it, or if the item is actually garbage.** Don't be a Susie; your first instinct is always the right one. When you find something that you want to keep, but it does not belong in that area, place it in the DOES NOT BELONG bin.

Be ruthless. **When it comes to purging, I like to say, when in doubt, toss it out!**

Once that area has been sorted, take the DONATE bin immediately to your car. This stops you from going back through it later and undermining your hard work. Trust yourself. If you decided to donate it during the sorting process, trust that you don't need it anymore. Now take a few minutes to put the DOES NOT BELONG stuff away in the proper home, and finish up by emptying the garbage and putting away your KEEP bin. Now you are ready to start all over again in another space!

Time Capsule Method

Some people struggle more than others with letting things go. We cover the many reasons **why it is so hard to let go** in "The Burden of Guilty Clutter" chapter, but for now, I wanted to talk about a really effective way of helping you learn **The Power of Purging.**

Eventually, purging your unloved and unwanted items will feel amazing and become a natural part of your everyday routine. It can make you feel lighter, energized, and help you fall in love with your home all over again. For some people, though, it takes some practice to get there.

When you are undecided about whether to keep something or not, don't stress yourself out over it. Let me tell you, everyone struggles in the beginning. Purging is stressful. We can't help but wonder, what if I need this again? I have to be honest with you, I don't regret anything I have ever purged, but in my experience, this is something that is best learned all by yourself.

I want the experience of de-cluttering and organizing your home to be positive and rewarding. It should make you feel exhilarated, not stressed out. If purging is causing you anxiety, let's take a step back and settle somewhere in the middle. This is where the Time Capsule Method comes in.

Get some boxes or large totes and place all of the things you are not sure about inside. Be sure to clearly label the outside with everything you have packed up. Once the box is full, create a **"If not opened by: _____"** label. I recommend choosing a date six months in the future. Now store that box somewhere out of the way, but also somewhere you could access just in case you do need something from inside. The basement, laundry room, or garage is a great spot to store your time capsules.

Ninety-nine percent of the time you will not need anything you have packed up. Honestly, once those things are out of your sight, you will probably forget all about them! **What this method does is give you peace of mind that if you do need something you have purged, you can simply go get it out of the box without much effort.**

In six months (or maybe longer if you have completely forgotton about your bins), when you stumble across your time capsules, it will be painless to get rid of them. Anything left inside you will KNOW you haven't used or needed in the past six months, and you will realize you haven't even missed them at all. **Don't even open the box! Take it directly to your car and drop it off at your favorite donation spot.** This method removes any stress and indecision from your de-cluttering process, and makes purging in the future (without needing a time capsule) much easier.

I love using this method in the kitchen. Almost everyone has small kitchen appliances we never use. **That rice cooker, the bread maker, or that food processor that have been collecting dust are taking away valuable space that can help you create a clutter-free kitchen!** Create some Time Capsules in your kitchen today. Pack up those extra mugs you never use, the unused appliances taking up too much space, and all of those random, extra Tupperware lids you have (come on, I know you have them). Pack up the unused things in your kitchen cupboards and make room for all the things that are sitting on your counter. Your kitchen is not only going to look better, but it is going to make preparing meals so much easier.

So grab some empty boxes or large totes, make some "expired by" labels, and make purging as painless as possible.

The One In / One Out Rule

This purging strategy works really well for the logical Cricket, and it is a perfect way to practice maintenance once your home is organized and clutter-free. I also use the method with my children for birthdays and Christmas, as it makes purging a tear-free experience for my kids.

The concept is so simple, but sometimes the simplest ideas are the most effective. The One In/One Out Rule states that whenever you bring something new into your home, you MUST get rid of one thing of equal size. If you buy a new shirt at the mall, you must purge an old one before you put the new one away.

This concept works especially well for small children. Before you open a new toy for them, they must choose an old toy to donate to another child. This method not only teaches children how to maintain a manageable amount of belongings, but it also shows them the joy of donating and giving to others.

Whenever my kids ask me to open the box of some new toy, I tell them they need to go and pick an old toy to give to another little boy or girl first. Usually, getting kids to give up their toys is like pulling teeth, but when they have a brand new toy they get to open, finding an old one to donate is a piece of cake!

This strategy takes practice to become a habit, but once it does, it is a simple way to ensure that your home never gets too overwhelming again. **It is much easier to get rid of something old when you have just purchased something new.**

Box Out the Boxes

I feel it necessary to cover this issue because, not only have many of my clients struggled with this, but it was a major source of clutter in my home at one point as well.

Boxes. Empty Boxes. Now, if you don't have any idea why empty boxes would be a clutter issue, you are lucky. My husband used to keep the empty boxes for everything we purchased. When we got married and moved into our first home, we had to buy a lot of new things. Our first home was a tiny 900 square feet, and we didn't have a garage or a lot of storage space. Still, Joe insisted we keep the empty boxes for everything just in case we had to return it. We had dozens and dozens of empty boxes in our laundry room just sitting there, collecting dust. When we finally replaced our old tube TV with a 48-inch flat screen, he insisted we keep the box for that as well. Have you ever seen a television box? It was literally 5 feet by 2 feet and we had zero place to store this thing. I had no choice. I strapped that giant box to the ceiling with bungee cords. I can only shake my head as I look back at myself during that time. Everyday, I walked under that giant box strapped to the ceiling, like it was a completely normal thing to do.

I know we were not alone either. I once bought a stereo from a man online, and when I went to pick it up, he had a "box room." I've never in my life seen anything like it. This guy had an entire room in his home dedicated to empty boxes. The walls were lined with shelving and the shelves were filled with hundreds of empty boxes. Now, there has got to be something better he could have used that space for!

A few months after I had strapped the TV box to our ceiling, I actually had to return something to the store. I can't even remember what it was I was returning, but I do remember asking the clerk if I actually needed the box in order to return something. Her answer changed my life forever: **"No!!! You do not need to keep the original packaging in order to return an item, just the receipt.** For some warranties you need to keep the bar code from the box, but the box itself is never necessary."

That day I pulled all of the manuals out of those empty boxes, stapled the receipts to them, and put the manuals and warranties in my new warranties basket. I took down the television box from the ceiling and recycled dozens of other empty boxes, gaining back some much needed storage space in my home!

So let go of the empty boxes you are holding on to and make room for the important belongings in your life.

Get Started Today

No matter what your home currently looks like, whether it is neat and tidy or a cluttered mess, we can all find items that we no longer need to keep. Purging is the perfect way to kick-start your organizing journey, and you can do a quick Garbage Bag Therapy or 21 Item Toss right now! Before you start reading the next chapter, take just a few short minutes and feel the Power of Purging today!

CHAPTER FOUR

Find the Valuable Real Estate in Your Home

Sometimes the biggest reason that we can't seem to stay organized is that the places we store our items are not **the places that they should actually be stored.**

In the beginning of this book I talked about using the acronym SPACE to properly organize your home. In the last chapter, we covered "P is for Purging," and in this chapter, we are going to talk about the importance of implementing "A is for Assign" in order to stay organized for good.

You're going to have to bear with me on this concept. I find it ridiculously hard to explain on paper, but I will try my absolute best not to bore the bananas out of you.

I think the best way to try and explain this is to just drop a truth bomb on you: we are all lazy. Now, I'm not talking about laziness in the laying-on-the-sofa-in-stained-sweat-pants-all-day kind of

way. What I mean is, when we're done using something and we have to walk all the way to the other side of the house to put it away, nine times out of ten, we'll set it aside to put away later.

When it comes to assigning a proper home for our belongings, almost all of us have already started off on the wrong foot. Most of the time, we have assigned our belongings a home in this situation:

You just moved to your new place. You're tired and overwhelmed and all you want to do is get the boxes emptied as quickly as possible. You open closets and cabinets and start unpacking everything, designating spots and putting stuff away. You may even have friends and family helping you to unpack, with little or no input on where you would like your things put. Usually, once everything has been put away, that is how it will remain…for years…whether it was the most logical or functional spot or not.

It is impossible to pick the best and most functional home for your belongings before you have even had a chance to live in and function in the space.

Just because your wine glasses are currently stored in the cupboard above your refrigerator doesn't mean that you have to keep them there forever, especially if a glass of wine with dinner every night is the only way eating with a picky toddler is bearable.

I cannot tell you how many times I have had conversations with friends, family, and clients that go something like this:

(Random person in my life): "I need your help organizing. My house is too small and I have no place to store all of my kid's toys."

(Me): "Why don't you try putting some in that closet right there in the living room beside where the kids like to play with their toys?"

(Random person in my life): "That closet is full of cleaning supplies."

(Me): "Why don't you relocate the cleaning supplies somewhere else?"

(Random person in my life): "Because that is where the cleaning supplies go."

(Me): Face Palm

Your stuff is not super glued into place. You can move it around and you should.

Relocating your items and rearranging your belongings in order to better fit the needs of your family and your home is a critical part of the organizing process.

It is ok to move things around.

You will more than make up the time you spend moving things around with each and every extra step that you'll save putting those things away.

So, how do you find out the best place to store all of your things? You start by first IDENTIFYING THE VALUABLE REAL ESTATE in your home.

The valuable real estate in your home are the areas that are the easiest to access. In your kitchen, the bottom shelf of your upper cabinets and the top drawers in your lower cabinets are the valuable real estate. If you are storing Christmas mugs (that are used once a year) on your lower shelf of your upper cabinets, you are wasting that valuable space.

In order to stay organized, your home has to be more than just a clean and clutter-free looking space. It needs to be functional. I'm sure you have heard this wonderful organizing mantra before: **"Everything in it's place and a place for everything."** While this is what it takes to have an organized home, it's having a truly functional home that keeps it staying neat and organized forever.

To have a functional home, one that practically cleans itself, you need to make sure that all the items you use every day are in the easiest to access place in the most high traffic areas of your home.

Here is the issue in a nutshell: **if something is hard to put away, we probably just won't do it.** We will set it aside and pile it up to be put away "later." It isn't just how hard something is to put away that affects the function of your home, either; it's also how long it takes you to put those things away.

If your dishes and utensils are not in the cupboard and drawer closest to the dishwasher, then putting away the dishes is going to eat up more of your precious time than it needs to. Even if it is just walking a few extra steps every day, all of those extra steps can add up to a lot of wasted time and energy.

I know that you may be thinking, but exercise is good! Okay, fine, exercise is good, but if you could add up all of that wasted time you spend on unnecessary effort, you could have so much more real time left over each day to spend exercising in ways you actually enjoy.

The best way to really describe this concept is to give you some examples.

When we moved into our current home I was over-the-moon excited to have a ginormous playroom for my kids. I filled it with all of their toys and games and I created an awesome art station for them—complete with an easel and everything they could ever want to get their "art" on.

The playroom seemed like the logical place to store all of their art supplies, but for some reason, our kitchen counter was always filled with piles of coloring books and crayons. Every day I would pile up their art supplies and eventually carry them back to the playroom, but the next day, the kids would carry everything back up so they could color in the kitchen again.

For our home, my kids designated the kitchen as the spot where they liked doing arts and crafts. As much as I loathed those piles of art supplies on my kitchen counter every day, no matter how many times I cleaned it up, the piles would just end up right back there again before I knew it.

If I described my ideal vision for how my kitchen would function, a coloring spot would not be on the list. Sometimes, though, your home and your family just have their own unique way of functioning, whether you like it or not. Instead of fighting the piles of art supplies, I worked with that clutter to create a home for it right where it was used the most. I cleaned out a few drawers in my kitchen that were storing aprons, place mats, and other stuff that was hardly used, and I relocated those things to a hall closet. Now we have three art and homework drawers right in our kitchen island, and those piles of clutter are a thing of the past.

Take a look at your "piles" around your home. Odds are, they are piled where they are because you or your family members are "waiting" to put the things away until "later." If you have to wait until later to put those things away, that usually means that the home for those things is not as convenient as it could be.

One of my very first clients struggled with paper clutter, and hired me to help them design a system that would finally free them of the piles of paper on their kitchen counter.

Because it was one of my first times ever organizing someone else's home,

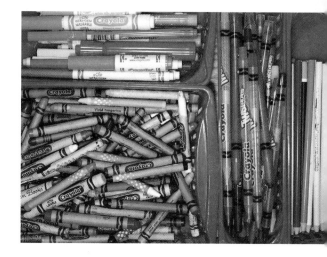

I made the mistake of listening to what the clients thought they wanted, instead of listening to what their home was telling me. This busy family had two full-time working parents and two adorable young children. Their two-story home was tidy and beautifully decorated, but the small kitchen had limited workspace and most of it was buried under mounds of mail, notes, and school papers.

I suggested we create a **Kitchen Command Center** to organize all of their paper, but they were adamant that they wanted the system to be in their home office, which was located on the second floor. **Sometimes, what we think is the ideal function for our home isn't necessarily the best option.** I spent six hours creating a beautiful filing system in their home office for all of their paperwork, complete with custom labels and hanging baskets for each of their children's school papers on the wall. My clients were thrilled and they assumed that their paper clutter was a thing of the past.

It wasn't even two weeks later when I received a call from them. Their kitchen counters were full of papers again, and they wanted me to come back and help them design a different system. This time, I had to get real with them.

I asked the parents to describe their daily routine when they came home from work every day. After work, the mom would pick up their children from daycare and grab the mail as she came in the front door. She would set the mail down on the kitchen island (which was just feet from the entrance) and help the kids unpack their backpacks (again, in the kitchen). The kids would have a snack and work on their homework at the kitchen table while she started dinner. About twenty minutes later, the dad would return home from work and drop his computer and files on the counter and start helping with dinner.

Their evenings were a blur of after-school activities and bedtime routines, and before they knew it, the parents were waking up the next morning to a kitchen counter full of paper again.

So why wasn't their home office paper system working? Because it wasn't a convenient spot; no one is going to take time out of his or her hectic schedule to put away papers all the way up the freaking stairs every night. The office wasn't the natural place that they stored or used those papers, the kitchen was. Therefore, the kitchen was the best spot to assign a paper organizing system.

The mom was not happy with this idea at all. She was convinced that, in no way, did she have space in their kitchen for anything else. She was also a Ladybug, so she hated the idea of seeing her paper filing system out in the open every day. I offered to set up a kitchen system that she could try for two weeks, and if she still didn't like it, I would come back and relocate and reorganize everything for free.

After peaking and snooping inside the cabinets, I found a bread maker, rice cooker, stand up mixer and a blender that were covered in dust and were obviously not being used. In such a small kitchen, storing unused items was a huge space waster. We moved these items to the basement, moved some things around, and freed up a large upper cabinet right above the island. I moved their mail sorting system into the cabinet and hung cork boards on the inside of the cabinet doors for messages and important papers. I moved the school paper baskets from the office and hung them in the kitchen instead, with a dry erase calendar mounted above.

My clients were less than impressed; this wasn't the system they had envisioned for their home at all. If Yelp was around back then, I would have been given a bad review for sure.

It was just a week later when the mom called me to let me know that their paper clutter was finally gone and that she loved the system now that they had been using it for awhile. I didn't slap her with a giant "I told you so," but the experience did help me become a much better organizer.

It's important to understand the flow of your home. It's also important to understand that sometimes creating "lazy organizing systems" isn't a bad thing. **Life is hard enough; you don't get extra bonus points for making things more difficult than they need to be.**

Let's adapt the motto, Work Smarter, Not Harder, when it comes to organizing our homes!

If you're always reading books in the living room, put a basket beside your reading chair to store some of your favorite books. If your kids never put their shoes away in the front hall closet, put a basket

at the front door just for them! Do you always toss your gently worn jeans and sweaters on top of your dresser? Just install some hooks behind your bedroom door for all of those dirty-but-not-dirty-enough-to-wash-yet clothes.

Your kitchen is by far the **most valuable real estate** in your entire home, and everything you store in there should be used often. The items you use every day should be in the easiest to access areas of your kitchen; store things where you use them the most, like pots and pans beside the stove and drinking glasses beside the sink. There is no reason why you can't store occasional kitchen items, like big soup pots or roasting pans, in some other storage area of your home in order to free up space for items you use often, like the toaster.

A few years ago, I was visiting my in-laws' home, and I felt the urge to organize. Their house is always really clean and gorgeous, but they store their stuff in the weirdest possible places. My mother-in-law is short, like five-foot-nothing on her tippy toes kind of short. She has exactly two shelves in her upper cabinets she can reach without a stool…two. One of these shelves was dedicated to drinking glasses and mugs, which makes sense, but the other one was used for her spices.

This may seem like a reasonable spot for spices, except my mother-in-law never uses spices when cooking, like ever. So, in her kitchen, where she can only reach two areas of upper cabinets, she uses one of those areas to store something she never uses.

I relocated the spices and was trying to decide what to put in this newly empty shelf, the **most valuable real estate in her kitchen.** She uses plates and bowls daily, but they were kept in the pantry (don't get me started) and it worked for them, so I left those there. When I asked her what else she uses **every single day,** she said that both her and my father-in-law drink coffee and tea multiple times a day. This empty shelf was the perfect spot to store their coffee, K-Cups, and tea, because it was directly above her Keurig, kettle, and coffee maker!

"Where is your coffee now?" I asked. Her response: "In the bathroom closet." I kid you not. I almost peed myself laughing. I would never have laughed at a client, but my in-laws and I have a great relationship… they laugh at me all the time!

Because the kitchen was filled the day they moved in and they had extra space in their bathroom closet, it seemed completely normal to walk back and forth across the house multiple times a day, each time they wanted a hot beverage… all the while storing things they never, ever used right above the coffee maker. You may be shaking your head, thinking that is crazy, but I can promise you, there are spots in your own home where you are doing the exact same thing.

Let's look at some easy techniques to help you find your valuable real estate and assign proper homes for your things.

Listen to your home's clutter - Take a look at your piles to get a really good idea of what items in your space are currently hard to put away. Even if the home for those items is in the same room and close by, it may still not be a convenient enough spot to use regularly. I see this a lot with teenagers. "Why won't he put his dirty clothes in the basket? Why does he just throw them on the floor?" Try moving the basket out of his closet and beside where he usually tosses his dirty clothes. Voila, the basket will get used and the floor will be clean! Lazy? Yes, but sometimes working with your laziest traits can create the most functional and effective solutions.

Get in the zone - Almost every room can be broken into different zones based on different activities and functions each room has. Perhaps your living room is used for watching television, a kid play area, and a place where you do your crafts. Set up zones in your living room that store all of the things you need for those different activities. Have one section dedicated to toy storage, another just for watching television, and use a rolling storage unit to house all of the craft supplies you are using for your current project.

Work Smarter, Not Harder - When trying to make your home as functional as possible, you have to listen to your inner lazy child! Try to set up your space so that you have to do as little work as possible to maintain it. I do a lot of little DIY projects all the time, and I'm constantly dragging tools back and forth from the garage. One day I had a lazy light bulb moment: why not store all my most-used tools in a tool box in the hall closet beside my kitchen? My kitchen counter is where I usually fix little broken things, replace batteries, and do small DIY projects. It made perfect sense to keep my tools close by. I no longer have piles of tools on my kitchen counter that need to be carried out to the garage.

Do the Tango - Reassigning a lot of your belongings will be work, I can't lie about that. Once you move your plates to the cabinet above the dishwasher, you'll need to reassign the stuff that was already in that cabinet to a more logical spot, and so on and so forth. You can easily dance your stuff all around the house finding the most functional homes, and sometimes that tango can seem to be a never-ending song. **Let me assure you, rearranging your things in order to make them easier to put away is worth every single second you spend doing it.** Not only will you always find unwanted items you can toss or donate along the way, but you will also be left with a clean and functional space that will be effortless to keep that way.

Remember, don't be afraid to dance those rarely used items you still want to keep into the garage or other storage area in order to free up valuable real estate for the things you use all the time.

Hopefully I have made this "A is for Assign" concept easy to understand. By setting up systems that allow you to be a little lazier, you're going to save time and effort and be able to enjoy a clutter-free home for life. Start reassigning today!

CHAPTER FIVE

Contain the Clutter

I am so excited about this chapter! We are finally to the fun stuff:containers. I realize in an earlier chapter I mentioned buying containers was the **biggest organizing mistake** (and it is), but buying containers is only a mistake when you try to use them before you have sorted, purged, and assigned a space for them to go. Containers can only be used properly when you know exactly what is going in them and you know the size and shape you'll need for the space.

My sister is a container-buying junkie. She is forever coming home with new Rubbermaid totes or storage containers with the best intentions of getting her home organized. While I share her obsession for buying bins and baskets, sometimes unused or misused containers can actually make a clutter problem much worse. In my sister's case, her busy family often uses containers for quick clean-ups by filling them with random clutter in order to tidy the house fast. While this does make her home clean and tidy in the short term, all of those filled and mixed up totes only lead to missing items and much more work in the long run.

So how do we use containers to get our house organized? We start by understanding our organizing style. Once you know what ClutterBug you are, you can better understand which type of storage bins and baskets will work best for you. Butterflies need clear or brightly colored containers in order for them to work, while Ladybugs need baskets and bins that will make everything inside hidden from sight. I will give you more tips on buying containers that work best for the different organizing styles throughout this chapter.

Next you need to know exactly what is going in the bins, so you know what size of container to purchase. You'll also need to measure the spot where it will be used in order to make sure that the container will fit. **Nothing is worse than buying a bunch of drawer dividers only to come home and discover they are too tall for your drawers.** I've been there, done that. I had to learn the hard way (multiple times) to always measure first and bring my tape measure with me to the store when buying organizing supplies.

We are now to the part of the journey where we can really transform your home. Not only do containers keep your belongings separate and easy to find (and put away), but they can also really customize your space and turn a boring closet into something personal and really beautiful.

Maybe I'm a huge nerd, but there is something so ah-inspiring about opening up a closet and seeing rows and rows of pretty colored, labeled bins and baskets. **More than just being eye-pleasing, containers can double or even triple your storage, too.** If you are like me and tend to hold on to too much stuff, the right containers can keep even the biggest ClutterBug neat and tidy.

That really is the key, the right containers. My husband and I have very different organizing styles. I'm a Ladybug, so I like to hide everything away and visual clutter can stress me out. That being said, it doesn't bother me in the least to have things a jumbled mess when they are out of sight, like inside drawers and closets. My husband, on the other hand, is a Cricket. He likes to make thousands of neat little piles all over the house with the things he hasn't put away yet. It makes his skin crawl to have things shoved randomly inside a drawer, as he needs things to have a proper home before he will put them away. This combination of Cricket and Ladybug used to create a hilarious and never-ending game of, "Cas, where did my pile go?" and my usual response of, "Did you check all of my hiding spots?" Poor Joe. I was constantly playing hide-the-pile and I rarely remembered where I had hidden it. We are a work in progress, but we have come a long way over the years. While we still do occasionally play our fun little game of hide-and-seek, we now have many organizing solutions and container-compromises that work for both of us.

The biggest battle in our home was paper. Paper clutter is something that almost every household struggles with. The biggest reason? A lack of an effective organizing system that works for everyone who is using it. For me, I like all of my paper filed and hidden out of sight, so a pretty accordion file folder is my go-to for all of my personal filing.

Unfortunately, this system doesn't work for our shared family papers, because my husband needs to see the papers out until he is finished with them. My filing system never worked for him, because if he didn't see the papers as a visual reminder, he would forget all about them. His preferred paper solution was neat piles on the desk until he can create detailed and organized binder systems or scan them into his computer. It wasn't until we found the right container that worked for both of us that our paper

battles finally came to an end. For us, a vertical magazine holder was the perfect solution and compromise for both of our styles. The to-do papers were off the desk and stored in pretty file folders (which made me happy), but because they were vertical and clearly labeled, they were really visible for my husband too. Our vertical action file is the perfect way to keep our ongoing paper clutter in check.

Here is an easy reminder for organizing papers: Vertical is Visible, Horizontal is Hidden. When you pile paper horizontally, it is hard to see and remember what is in the pile. Storing papers vertically will make them visible and easier to access.

I still use my preferred method for my own personal paperwork and he uses his own piling method for his, but for our shared action files, this vertical hanging system really works for us both. You will probably have to discover the art of container-compromise in your own home, especially if you live with different organizing styles. If your family is in a constant battle over clutter, no one ever truly wins. **Trying to force others to organize the way you organize is pointless; you can't change their natural style anymore than they can change yours.** By finding systems and containers that work for everyone, your home can finally run efficiently and stay tidy for good.

Let's get started in your home right now. **The easiest place to begin and the best way to see the biggest impact from containers is in your bathroom or linen closet.** If you don't have a bathroom or linen closet, choose the spot where you currently store your toiletries and other extra bathroom products. My linen closet is teeny-tiny, so using containers is key to keeping it organized.

Begin by pulling everything in the closet out and going through the SPACE steps we talked about earlier in this book. Sort everything into like piles, such as all lotions together, all first aid supplies together…you get the idea, right? Next, purge expired or unused items. You now have to decide how you want this closet to function and what you want kept in there. Just because you have always kept your Christmas wrapping paper in your bathroom closet doesn't mean it has to stay there forever! What things do you use the most? Assign those things the middle, or easiest to reach shelf, with the least used items on the very top or bottom shelves.

Here is where the fun part begins! Now we get to choose the containers that we will use to store our sorted items. For me, the dollar store is my go-to place for plastic bins and containers. They have a huge selection of various shapes, sizes, and colors for a fraction of the price you will pay anywhere else. **I would much rather spend money on the things going inside the container instead of on the container itself.** Don't forget to also shop your home; you may have unused or misused bins or baskets that would be perfect for your closet without having to buy anything new. Even empty boxes or recycled containers can be used for organizing your space in a pinch!

My advice on containers for your toiletries is to use open containers that do not have a lid, especially if you have multiple styles in your home. While stacked containers will give you much more storage space, taking the time to unstack and re-stack them every time you need something will only work well for Crickets and some Bees. Open containers work well for everyone, and by labeling the containers very clearly, even Butterflies will be able to put everything away with ease.

Macro Versus Micro-Organizing

This seems like the perfect place to talk to you about **macro versus micro-organizing.** Macro-organizing is organizing your belongings into big categories, like all of your medications put together in one large bin or basket. Micro-organizing is when you break that category down further, like all pain-relievers together in one container and all of your allergy medicine in another. Remember to be aware of both your own style and your family's style when organizing your space. Crickets and Bees like things to be really micro-organized, and when the system is set up, they can easily maintain it long-term. Butterflies and Ladybugs, on the other hand, tend to prefer macro-organizing and can sometimes have trouble using micro-organized systems well.

My advice? Everyone should start by macro-organizing the space first. You can always go back and micro-organize at a later date, when you have some extra free time. The problem with micro-organizing first is that, not only is it much more time-consuming, but it can create a system that is just organizing overkill. Yes, you can be over-organized! **If your system is complicated to use, you probably won't use it.**

I made the mistake of micro-organizing everything when I first began my journey from cluttered to clean. Not only did I micro-organize my own home, but I made the same mistake with some of my clients' homes as well. **I believed that having a really sorted and detailed system was what being organized was all about, but I was very wrong.** Being organized is about having a space that is so efficient and functional, it is easy and effortless to maintain.

I'll never forget the first time I organized a bathroom closet for a client, and the results, while beautiful and very organized, were short-lived (as in, a few days later, it was a disaster again). I followed up with the family a few weeks after I had organized their main floor, and the mom admitted that they were not able to keep it clean and tidy. **She was upset and felt like a failure, which means of course, I had failed her as a professional organizer.** Organizing systems should be easy and fail-proof when done properly; the fact they were struggling to maintain the new system was my fault, not theirs.

So where did I go wrong? **I had over-organized their home.** I purchased dozens of clear stacking shoebox containers from the dollar store and sorted everything into like categories for the family. I had bins for pain relievers and different bins for cold medication. I had a bin just for extra bars of soap and another just for extra toothbrushes and toothpaste. Each bin was labeled and stacked neatly, and while the closet did look pretty and Pinterest-worthy, it was a pain in the butt to get anything you needed. If you had a headache, you needed to unstack a few bins, open the lid to get what you needed, put the bottle back, close the lid, and re-stack the bins. When I returned to their home and opened the closet, there were dozens of products just set loosely back on random shelves in front of those neatly stacked bins. Putting those things away was just too annoying a task, so no one bothered.

You may be thinking that this is just pure laziness. If that thought crossed your mind, you are probably a Cricket (or a DragonFly, in which case, why are you still reading this book?). **For the rest of us, lazy or not, if something is hard to put away, we just are not going to do it.**

So, I re-organized the closet for them (yes, I did this a lot in the beginning, which is probably why Professional Organizing is not a money-making venture for me). This time I used a more macro approach and used large baskets without lids. One basket for first aid, one for extra products, one for medications, and so on. While this method

was not nearly as organized as it was the first time, it was much easier to use. The family could reach in a basket, grab what they needed, and then toss it back in when they were done. No fuss, no muss. I made sure to clearly label the baskets, so it was obvious which basket contained what, and the family had no problem maintaining the new, less organized system. Sometimes, a more lazy approach to organizing is actually the best approach.

There isn't one area of my home that doesn't utilize containers. Every drawer, every cupboard, every closet, and every shelf is lined with baskets and bins. **Containers are really the secret to organization.** If you have ever wondered why some people are able to keep their homes neat and tidy all the time, I can assure you, they are probably container junkies (or minimalists...but it's hard to get messy when you have nothing to leave out).

Here is why containers are the key; they contain your stuff (I have an overwhelming urge to insert an "LOL" here, my poor editor). Having your things sorted and contained in a bin or basket means they will stay sorted and not get all jumbled and mixed up over time. They also ensure that when you need something, you will always know exactly where it

is and it will take just seconds to grab it. **Your container is the home for your belongings.**

So let's contain some stuff! Create a bin for cords, one for lightbulbs, and another for batteries. Measure that junk drawer and get some dollar store drawer dividers to finally get it sorted out! I love storing my K-Cups in a basket inside the coffee cupboard in my kitchen. After years of trying different fancy organizers, I found that a dollar store basket held the most and was the easiest to use!

If you are a Butterfly, be sure to use clear bins or some bright and fun colors that you love and find beautiful; a brown basket is not going to inspire you to put your things away when you are done with them. If you are a Bee, invest is some large totes or banker boxes to use as project boxes; store all of the supplies you need for an ongoing project in these and clearly label them! Crickets, you can get away with stacked and really sorted organizing systems. Bento box-style organizers are a dream come true for you, especially for small things like tools and office supplies.

I now try to stick to a container color scheme for my home, and I wish I would have done this from the beginning. While I'm not about to replace perfectly good bins and baskets with new ones just for aesthetics, it does look much better to have your closets and cabinets look somewhat coordinated. Now, when I shop at the dollar store for new containers, I try to stick with red and white for my kitchen, aqua for the girls' bedroom and blue for my son's room. The dollar store has so many color options; you can easily pick your favorite and make your space look beautiful and personalized on a small budget.

The most important step when containing your clutter is labeling those containers. Labels are truly magic. Not only will labels ensure that everything is easy to find in your home, they also ensure that everything gets put away in the correct spot as well. I even label inside my refrigerator. Yep, I'm crazy like that. My labeled fridge means I never have to search for the ketchup because my family and I always put it back in its labeled home.

My husband makes fun of me for my labeling obsession, but I have seen first hand how the simple act of labeling a container can actually encourage people to put things away properly. It really is magic! A child who struggles to clean up their toys will suddenly have no problem once the toys bins are labeled with pictures. A messy office can be transformed with a clearly labeled action folder. I have no idea why it works, but trust me, it does. You and your family will actually start putting things away much more frequently when the spot where those things belong is clearly labeled. I know there have been numerous studies, but instead of me spending hours trying to locate those stats for you, just take a leap of faith on this one and give labeling a try.

My favorite type of labels? Big fat juicy ones (ok, well maybe not juicy). Bigger is better when it comes to labeling your containers. I love using chalkboard labels, from the dollar store of course, along with a chalk pen so they won't rub off without water. You can simply wipe with a damp cloth and re-label whenever things get moved around.

I also love creating custom labels on my computer, and I make picture labels for my son, who can't quite read yet. If you want to invest in a label maker, they are perfect for labeling small things, like file folders or the tops of your spice lids!

So organize something today! Pick one small area of your home, a drawer or a shelf perhaps, and sort, purge, and contain it right now! Finish it up with some labels and sit back and watch the magic unfold. **The small space you organize today will be the start of your war on clutter, and containers are going to be your secret weapon!**

Chapter Six

The Burden Of Guilty Clutter

The best way to get rid of clutter is to purge and purge often. That being said, letting go of our belongings can be really hard sometimes. For a lot of people (including myself), some of the most difficult things to part with we don't even like (or want) in our homes in the first place. You may be thinking, why would anyone have a hard time letting go of stuff they don't even like? However, the struggle is real, and I would bet it's happening to you, too. As silly as it sounds, many of us hold onto things, not out of love, but out of guilt. I like to call these things "guilty clutter."

Guilty clutter is unwanted items we are holding onto out of obligation. Maybe it's that expensive treadmill you haven't used in five years or your great grandmother's china that was passed down to you. We all have unloved and unused things taking up valuable space in our homes.

Here's the bottom line: nothing good can come from holding onto unwanted stuff. **This fear that we are giving away hard-earned money, hurting someone's feelings, or disrespecting our loved ones who have passed away is all in our heads.** It's time we overcome that fear and open ourselves up to the joy that comes from letting go.

Let's talk about the different types of guilty clutter and the ways we can overcome the need to keep it. I promise you, letting go will feel so much better than holding on.

Sentimental Clutter

I wanted to jump right in with the hardest kind of clutter to let go of, the touchy-feely kind. For you, it may be your grandmother's beloved china dishes or those boxes of thirty-five-year-old baby clothes

in your attic. I'm not talking about the keepsakes you love and cherish and proudly display in your home; what I want to address is the stuff you feel you have to keep, even though you don't want to. **The sentimental clutter I'm talking about is usually forgotten and boxed up in your basement collecting dust, yet the thought of getting rid of it can still give you heart palpitations.**

Shortly after my husband and I had our third child, our son Milo, my mother-in-law brought over two huge totes filled with my husband's baby clothes she had kept all these years. My husband was born in the '80s and no clothing from this era should ever see the light of day again. I tried to contain my horror at the thought that she wanted my son to wear his father's old clothes. I mean, I'm no fashion snob, but thirty-year-old faded and musty smelling baby clothes look better in a box than on a baby. Still, it was fun going through the boxes and seeing all of the memories inside. The only problem was, these boxes were now mine to keep, and I had no storage space whatsoever to keep them in. **My sweet mother-in-law had just passed her guilty clutter onto me.**

I tried to politely suggest I just pick out a few pieces of clothing from the box and she could keep the rest, but she dropped a truth bomb on me so big that all I could do was laugh. "I don't want these in my house," she said sheepishly. "I have wanted to get rid of them for years, but I felt so guilty, so now I can give them to you."

Ummmm, thanks?

It's what we do. We keep our baby clothes and other sentimental keepsakes because we feel we "should" or that it is a "good parent" thing to do, and then we end up passing the buck onto our kids when they get older. Sometimes, we pass down our guilty clutter from generation to generation. By the time the youngest generation gets the stuff, it's so loaded with guilt, letting go of it would never be an option.

I'm not suggesting we never keep anything, or that it is wrong to hold onto mementoes, keepsakes, and baby items. I'm suggesting that keeping a few special pieces of clothing is a much better idea than keeping two boxes full. I am also suggesting that passing those few special pieces of clothing onto your children when they are grown should come with a disclaimer that, in no way, should they feel obligated to keep anything they don't want to.

A few years ago, I had a wonderful client who lived in a modest two-bedroom home with her husband. They had been saving for years with the dream of remodeling their home, and now that they were both recently retired, that dream was about to become a reality. The problem was, her home was so full of stuff they had no place to put anything during the remodel—hence why she had contacted me.

I decided to begin in the spare bedroom, because it was the fullest room in the house, with barely a path to get inside. The room was filled with dozens of stacked boxes, and they honestly had no idea what was in most of them. My first suggestion was, because you don't even know what is in the boxes, let's have them go to charity without even opening or looking inside. The terror in her face was all the answer I needed, and we spent the next week going through each and every one of those boxes.

Almost everything in that room was guilty clutter. She had a huge collection of salt and pepper shakers, that at one point, were displayed in her kitchen on endless shelves. She confessed she no longer wanted to display them and that, more than anything, she wanted a clean and modern-looking kitchen and home. As she unwrapped and looked through her collection, she gushed over the memories that each shaker brought her. She wanted to keep them all, but she didn't want them displayed.

This is the part of my job as a Professional Organizer I loathe. I know my clients need to let go of their unwanted things in order to have what they really want, but getting them to let go of the guilt is an emotionally draining process for everyone. After a while, my client began to understand that her salt and pepper shakers were not the physical memories she had attached to them; her memories she could hold onto forever. She realized that taking pictures of the shakers and keeping a photo album could allow her to keep those same memories, while letting go of the actual clutter. In the end, she kept only five sets out of over one hundred, and the rest were sold on eBay.

The best part of this particular organizing gig was the tears of relief my client shed when her spare bedroom was finally emptied. She now had a place for her daughter to sleep when she visited and a designated quilting space, something she had always dreamed of having. The money they received from eBay for the sale of her salt and pepper shakers was enough for her and her husband to get some expensive upgrades on their

remodel. My favorite of the entire process was that her reluctance to let go of guilty clutter was completely gone, and she was able to tackle the rest of her home without the fear and guilt she had before.

I could tell you dozens of stories, each one just as inspiring as the last, but instead I want to give you some easy tips that can help you get rid of that unwanted sentimental clutter in your home.

- You are not honoring your loved ones' memories by storing their prized possessions in a box in your basement or attic. You could honor them best by passing those items on to someone who would love and cherish them as much as your loved ones did.

- Physical items are not the memories themselves. Take photos of these special things and write down the memories you have attached to them. Create a photo album you can look at often, and let the physical stuff go to charity so that it can continue to make new memories elsewhere.

- Transform the unused items into something useful. I love the idea of having a baby blanket made out of old baby clothes, or making an accent pillow from your father's favorite t-shirt. **Transforming those things from the past into something beautiful and that you love today is a wonderful way to honor the memory.**

- Remind yourself that you don't want to burden your children with the keepsakes you are saving for them. I promise you, I am not sad my mother didn't give me boxes full of the artwork I made as a child. She did keep one small box of mementoes for me, which I thought was sweet, but even those are now items I feel obligated to also hold onto. **Be mindful not to pass on our guilty clutter to our loved ones.**

- Your collectibles are not worth as much as you think they are. If I had a dollar for every client that had a collection of Beanie Babies®, I could take a pretty sweet vacation somewhere exotic with the cash. People collect things, assume they are worth something, and hold onto the collection for years in the hopes of cashing in. In my experience, the collection is usually worth only a fraction of what it was hoped to be worth, and people are left resentful for having held onto it for so long. I would recommend checking out the prices on sites like eBay to get a good idea of what your collection is really worth, and see if it is worth the space it takes up in your home.

Just because your mother loved her Royal Doulton collection does not mean you have to keep it in your home after she is gone. Having unwanted clutter can cause you stress and resentment your loved ones would never want you to feel. Take pictures, rejoice in the memories, and then give or sell those items to someone who will give them the love they deserve. **Your home is your sanctuary and should be filled only with things you yourself love and cherish today, not items that were only loved in the past.**

Expensive Clutter

We have all made expensive purchases we later regretted, like my dust-collecting treadmill, but we also have expensive out-dated items that can be just as hard to part with. I can't tell you the number of clients I had who were storing old electronics or workout equipment in their basement, just because they couldn't bear to get rid of such high priced items.

Following into the same category as expensive clutter are all of those items people hold onto because "they may need them some day." No one wants to get rid of something and then have to purchase it again later when they need it, so the fear of spending unnecessary money causes some people to hold onto things they will likely never need again.

Unfortunately, sometimes we tend to think of our belongings as having the same value as the day we bought them. You may have spent one thousand dollars on your television ten years ago, but today you would be lucky to get one hundred dollars for it. **By storing it in your basement, you are not one thousand dollars richer; that money you spent on your TV is already long gone.** Holding onto expensive items out of fear of losing money can quickly escalate and turn your home into a cluttered mess.

For some people, letting go of unused items can feel like throwing away hard-earned cash. This fear is intensified in people who are struggling financially or have struggled in the past. I have even seen clients who had learned this hoarding behavior from their parents, even though they had never lived in poverty themselves.

Here are a few tips to help you let go of expensive clutter and stop seeing your belongings as the dollar amount you spent on them.

- Remember that the money you spent on your item is gone. You are not any richer because you store this item in your home, and you won't be poorer if you let it go.

- Selling your unused items through an online sale can really be a motivating way to purge. Just remember to price your things appropriately; any money you receive will be much more than you are making from it just collecting dust in your house.

- Ask yourself, what is the worst thing that can happen if I get rid of this item? Most of the time, our fear of letting go is completely unfounded. When we stop and think about worst-case scenarios, we usually find that it's really not that bad at all.

- Donate your unused things to a charity you can feel good about. Sure, you spent a hundred dollars on that sweater you've never worn, but keeping it in your closet is just a reminder of your mistake. That money is gone, and keeping the sweater in your closet isn't going to bring it back. Acknowledge your mistake and make it better by passing the sweater onto someone who will love it and wear it often. There are so many thrift stores that use your donations to help people right in your community.

- If you haven't used or needed something in twelve months, the odds are you never will. Holding onto things for someday only takes away from the things you need and use today.

- Keeping unused things is taking from you, not giving. It doesn't matter how much something cost when you bought it, if you aren't using it then it's taking up valuable space in your home for nothing. Not only is it taking away space, but those expensive items are making us feel bad and guilty every time we look at them; not to mention the stress that clutter can cause.

- Purging or donating your unused items is not being wasteful. It is more wasteful to have something collecting dust in your house instead of recycling it or passing it on to someone who will really use it.

Purging is by far the most difficult part of getting organized, and you will need to push yourself in order to see real results in your home. Just remind yourself of your end goal; a clean and clutter-free home.

You don't have to be a minimalist to get there, but you may need to work through some fears you have with regards to letting go. Do you see your belongings as memories? Do you worry that getting rid of your belongings is throwing away money? Are you afraid you may really need that item again one day? Letting go can be a tough process, but I can promise you, it does get easier. The more you purge, the less fear you will have and the easier it will become. Start small and enlist the help of a friend or family member you trust if you have to.

Keep reminding yourself your unused items are taking from you, not giving. Let go of the clutter that makes you feel guilt, shame, and sadness today.

Chapter Seven

Routines, To-Dos and Checklists...Oh My!

The final part of the SPACE organizing method is "E" for Evaluate. The truth is, now that you have organized your space, you will still have to do occasional tidying in order to keep it organized long term. I can almost hear the collective groan now. Let me reassure you, evaluating your space and making some small tweaks in order is accommodate new things coming into your home or adjusting systems that are not working will not take very long at all. I recommend working organizing maintenance into your regular cleaning schedule.

When I first starting doing the whole "adult" thing, I never had a cleaning schedule. I cleaned things when they looked dirty, and usually, I didn't clean very often or well, unless I knew someone was coming over. When company was coming over, look out, though—I went on a rampage cleaning and hiding clutter everywhere while screaming like some sort of she-beast. It would literally take me days to get the house ready for guests. **Here is some house cleaning wisdom I have discovered along the way; if you wait until your home already looks dirty to clean it, you've waited too long.**

The good news is, now that your home is organized, it will only take a fraction of the time to clean and tidy it. Even the most organized homes will still get messy from time to time. Just like your car needs regular maintenance to run efficiently and stay in good working condition, your home requires regular maintenance as well. I'm not just talking about emptying out the gutters or caulking around the windows, either; the best way to maintain your home is with good old soap and water. Home maintenance includes both regular cleaning as well as small repairs and preventative work. Unfortunately, our homes do not come with instruction manuals explaining exactly what we need to do in order to take care of it properly. Fortunately for you, I'm going to share some simple ways you can not only keep your home clean and tidy on a daily basis, but also keep it in tip-top shape for years to come.

There is one undeniable truth I have learned about life in my almost forty years on this planet: **becoming good at something requires practice.** I'm not a fan of practicing anything and I never have been. I get bored easily, and I'm convinced I have an actual allergic response to hard work. When I was young, our school had an annual talent show a bunch of my friends and classmates would partake in. Kids danced or sang or played the piano to my utter amazement. I, on the other hand, had zero talents to share. There had never been anything in my life I enjoyed doing enough to warrant doing it over and over again, except, of course, watching television.

Even as a young adult, I remained under the impression I was just born terrible at everything. Forget playing an instrument or a sport; I could barely manage the whole basic-necessities-of-life stuff.

I couldn't cook, clean my house or manage my money, and I had pretty much just chalked this up to the fact that I just wasn't good at that stuff. **While it is true people are born with some natural ability in different areas, for the most part, practice and self-discipline are the keys to success.**

If you, like me, struggle to keep your house clean, let me assure you: **we can fake it 'til we make it, especially in the housework department.** What I have discovered is that you can train your self-discipline muscle, and overtime, it will grow stronger and easier to use. The best way to train yourself? Committing to doing one small change in your life at the same time, each and every day. Whether that small change is a daily walk, playing an instrument, or spending a few minutes cleaning your house, with a little practice each and every day, this new addition to your life will become easier, and it can even become something you are really great at.

They say that it only takes **thirty days of repeating a new behavior in order for it to become a habit.** They also say, **a little bit of motivation gets you started, but habit is what keeps you going.** I'm not sure who "they" are, but I'm pretty sure that "they" are onto something here. I spent the first thirty years or so of my life making a habit out of being messy; thankfully, it only took thirty days of effort to create new habits that keep my home clean.

For me, it was just one new behavior that transformed my home from messy to clean literally overnight: my **Nightly Cleaning Routine.** I created a checklist of small chores that needed to be done each and every night, and I made sure I did the tasks on the checklist, no matter what. To keep me motivated, I had to make sure the chores took no longer than twenty minutes to complete, and no matter how tired or busy I may have been, I never went to bed without completing my nightly routine.

In the beginning, I had to force myself to do this every day. I have three small children, and as soon as they are in bed, the last thing I want to do is more housework. What I want to do is enjoy every single second of "Mommy alone time," but putting off those quick chores only creates even more work for me the next day. Getting myself to do anything I don't want to do requires a lot of inner nagging and bargaining. I basically have to parent myself. Just like I put on my mean Mom face and make my kids do their chores/homework before they can watch television or play, I parent myself the same exact way. Before I allow myself

to watch Netflix, craft, or have a bedtime snack, I force myself to do my nightly chores first.

So here is my **Nightly Cleaning Checklist.** Your routine may look different, but no matter what your living situation is, everyone needs a nightly routine in order to make having a clean and tidy home practically effortless.

- **Load the dishwasher**
  (5 minutes)
- **Wipe down the kitchen counters**
  (1 minute)
- **Wipe down the bathrooms**
  (1 minute)
- **Put away any clutter left out**
  (3 minutes)
- **Speed mop the floors**
  (5 minutes)
- **Put away one load of laundry**
  (5 minutes)

This simple list of daily chores had a huge impact on my home and my life. Waking up every morning to a clean house always feels so much better than waking up to a messy one. It really does set the tone for my entire day, and I feel happy and energized instead of overwhelmed and exhausted. I also find it so much easier to fall asleep at night, just knowing I've accomplished a little something and knowing I'll be waking up to a fresh and clean start the next day. The best part is because I do a little bit every night, my home never really gets overrun with clutter or grime anymore. These few minutes I spend each night save me hours of scrubbing in the long run.

The trick to having an effective routine and checklist is, of course, to write it down. There is something so motivating about checking items off a list, and just the simple act of creating a list makes you much more likely to accomplish your goals. **To-do lists and checklists are hands down the best tool to motivate you and keep you on track, no matter what the goal is you are working towards.**

So grab a piece of paper (or use some new fangled technology, like your phone) and create your nightly cleaning checklist right now! Make sure you only pick a few chores you would like to get done, and make sure your routine won't take you more than twenty minutes to complete. Make it a family routine and you can save even more time every day! Once your **Nightly Cleaning Routine** becomes a habit, it is time to create a twenty minute **Morning Cleaning Routine** as well. Here is mine:

- Make the beds
- Clean up kitchen
- Clean up bathrooms
- Put in one load of laundry

Yeah, it is pretty underwhelming, I know. It also doesn't have the same life-changing impact my nightly routine does, but it still makes a big difference to my day. When I take the time to make my bed (which really can be done in less than two minutes), I feel a boost of energy and motivation. Not only that, but my bedroom always looks so much better, so I'm way less likely to toss dirty clothes on the floor or leave other random junk on my bed during the day. It is a small effort with big rewards. The best part is how much nicer and more relaxing it feels to climb into a made bed at the end of a long day.

If you're not a bed maker, you are probably rolling your eyes right about now. I get it, I do. I used to belong to the why-make-the-bed-when-you-are-just-going-to-get-back-in-it-at-night club. It's just one of those "try it and you'll see the difference" kind of things you have to discover for yourself. Go ahead and create your own **Morning Cleaning Routine**, but no matter how rushed your mornings are, be sure to include making your bed.

You may be wondering how on earth you are actually going to stick to a morning and nightly routine, when you never have been able to do it consistently before. You may have tried in the past to force yourself to clean up the house every day, but life got in the way and you simply didn't keep it up. So, what will make this time different? This time, I'm going to give you a fail-proof plan of action that will ensure success. These steps will work for whatever type of to-do list or checklist you want to implement, and it will ensure that these goals you are setting for yourself will soon become a daily habit you no longer even think twice about doing.

Here are my WICKED **steps to daily goal setting success.** I grew up as a teenager in the nineties, where wicked meant a super-awesome good thing, not evil stepmother kind of bad. With that in mind, here are my wicked-awesome steps to daily goal setting success…yep, another acronym. I have a thing for acronyms.

W - Write It Down. Write yourself a to-do list with no more than six quick and easy tasks. Make these tasks really attainable, such as making the bed, not cleaning the bedroom. If cleaning the bedroom is your main goal, create a checklist with the steps you need in order to accomplish that goal, i.e., make the bed, clean off the dresser, put away clean clothes, wash dirty clothes, de-clutter other surfaces.

I - In Plain Sight. Place the list in a really visual spot so you see it often throughout the day. Having your list in plain sight will remind you of the tasks you want to accomplish and make you much more likely to actually get them done.

C - Check It Off. Actually check each item off or cross out each task as you complete them. There is something really motivating about physically checking off a completed task. And this feeling of accomplishment and pride will motivate you to check off the next task on the list.

K - Kick Your Own Butt. Be your own parent. If you are like me and have trouble self-motivating, think of yourself as your own parent and treat the situation as you would if you were asking your children to complete the list. Would you allow your kids to watch television before the list is complete? **I often tell myself to put on my big girl pants and just get the job done quickly, or bribe myself with a reward afterwards, like an extra thirty minutes of reading or television before bed.** You would be surprised at how a little tough love on yourself can make a big difference in your self-discipline.

E - Erase and Repeat. Slip your checklists into a clear plastic protective sleeve so that you can easily check off tasks with a dry erase marker and then wipe clean and start fresh again the next day. You can also use a dry erase memo board or chalkboard to keep track of your daily chores and checklists.

D – Don't Give Up. Are there days when you are going to forget, or be too sick, tired, or busy to do your new routine? Of course, but for each day that is missed, it is harder and harder to get back on top of things again. Shake off a missed day, don't give up, and get back

to your routine the next day. **The secret to having a clean house that never gets really dirty is to do just a little bit of cleaning every single day.**

For the first few weeks of my daily cleaning "training," my list had to be on the fridge and I had to physically check it off every night to keep myself from giving up. Now, I keep all of my cleaning and home maintenance lists in a binder, which I call my Household Management Binder. Today, all of my daily cleaning and weekly routines are such a habit, I no longer have to refer to the checklist, nor do I have to physically check off the list every day.

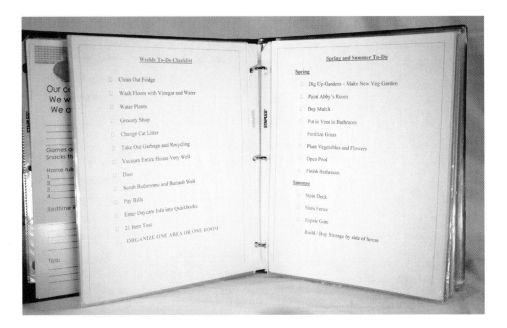

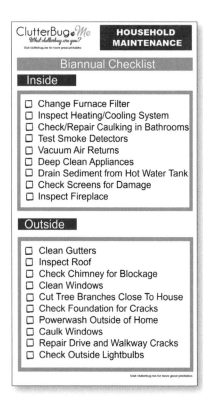

Besides my Daily Cleaning Checklist, I also have a Weekly Cleaning Routine. Here are the bare bones basic things I do each week to keep on top of housework.

Monday: Dust House

Tuesday: Vacuum and Mop

Wednesday: Deep Clean Bathrooms

Thursday: Do a 21 Item Toss

Friday: Wash All the Bedding and Towels

Your checklists are probably going to look completely different than mine, but just remember when creating your own that they are really easy and attainable. Your routines should fit your home and family's needs, and it should never feel overwhelming or too time consuming to complete. If you are looking for inspiration for creating your list or you want a pre-made list you can simply print out, the Internet is full of beautiful and free cleaning and home maintenance checklists you can use.

I will admit it, I may be a little gaga for lists, but that is only because they really do work. I have daily, weekly, monthly, and yearly home checklists I keep in my Household Management Binder. My binder is like an instruction manual for my home, and I really recommend you create one for yourself. You can download everything you need to make your binder from my website for free at: www.clutterbug.me/printables.

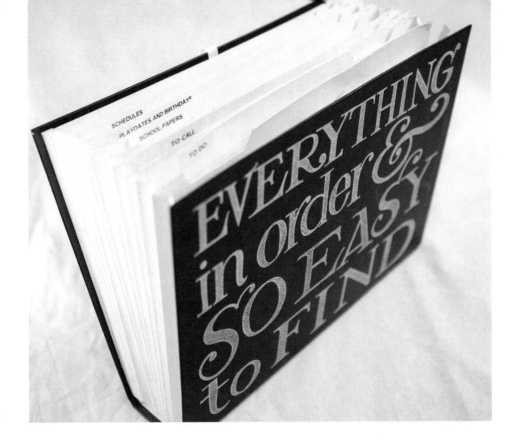

SCHEDULES
PLAYDATES AND BIRTHDAYS
SCHOOL PAPERS
TO CALL
TO DO

I also make lists for so much more than just cleaning my home, and it is those lists that keep me on track and productive throughout my day to day. I keep my family and household lists on the side of my fridge on what I call the Kitchen Command Center.

These include shopping lists, meal planning, and general home to-dos. In my office is where I keep my work related lists and checklists, and they have been crucial to the success of my blog and even getting this book written.

The Procrastination Problem

Here's the thing, I'm a procrastinator; not only do I leave important tasks to the absolute last minute, but I also often forget things I need to get done all together. I can't deny I'm a hot mess at best, but I would be an even bigger and hotter mess if it were not for my love of list making.

Right now, my daily work checklist includes responding to emails, researching new blog ideas, creating one blog post, video or podcast, and, of course, writing this book for at least one hour. My checklist always sits on my desk as a reminder of these daily tasks, but if it wasn't visible, I would most definitely forget to do one or all of them. Even if I didn't forget, the old me would most certainly start with the tasks that I enjoy the most (like researching, yeah Pinterest!) and I would procrastinate the jobs I didn't want to do (like write this book, because writing is way harder than I thought). My tendency to procrastinate the things I dislike would usually mean I'd have to rush to get them done (and never do them well), or I wouldn't even get to them at all. So how did I change my procrastinating ways? Honestly, it's a work in progress (just ask my editor), but I have come leaps and bounds.

The technique that helps me the most with my procrastination problem is an amazing and simple one, *Eat that Frog*. This technique is the entire basis of a bestselling book by the same name, *Eat That Frog*, by Brian Tracy. While I loved this book and I highly recommend this as the best method I've ever tried to stop myself from procrastinating, I can save you a little time and break down the book as:

"Mark Twain once said that if the first thing you do each morning is to eat a live frog, you can go through the day with the satisfaction of knowing that that is probably the worst thing that is going to happen to you all day long.

Your "frog" is your biggest, most important task, the one you are most likely to procrastinate on if you don't do something about it. It is also the task that can have the greatest impact on your life and results at the moment." – direct quote from *Eat That Frog* by Brian Tracy.

So that is basically it in a nutshell. Make yourself a list of all the things you need to do and then complete your "frog" first. For me, writing this book is definitely my frog due to an ongoing case of writer's block and a complete and utter lack of confidence in my ability as a writer. I tend to put off writing, despite the fact that completing this book is the one task that will bring me the greatest sense of accomplishment and have the greatest impact on my life as of this moment. When I make the effort to "eat my frog" first thing every morning, I never have to feel guilty about putting it off, and I don't have to worry about not getting it done at all.

> "The first rule of frog eating is this:
>
> **If you have to eat two frogs, eat the ugliest one first".**

If you find that you have more than one important task you need to accomplish in a day, always start with the one you are dreading the most. The rest of your day will seem like a piece of cake once you have checked that bad boy off your list.

I feel it necessary to admit to you that this chapter was even more difficult for me to write than the others, and here's why: while I am a crazy list maker and I never miss my nightly cleaning routine, I still struggle to get everything I want to accomplish done most days. I have things on my to-do lists that never seem to get done, and I have days when I feel as though I'm not accomplishing anything at all. **I literally procrastinated on this chapter about how to overcome procrastination and I am submitting it to my editor a half a week late.** You see the irony, right?

My point is, this book isn't about how to be some super efficient homemaker, or even about having a perfectly clean and organized home. Sometimes, your house is going to look like a dumpster exploded and that is totally normal. Sometimes you are going to feel like a disaster yourself, and you should never feel bad about that. Life is hard. Adulting is hard. Keeping a clean home can be hard, too. I have found a few tips and tricks that can make it a little bit easier, and this book is all about sharing those tips with you. Just remember, having a clean and organized home isn't about striving for perfection, it's about making your life easier and freeing up extra time for the things that really matter, like friends and family…and Netflix.

Laundry
the never ending story

This *Home* has
ENDLESS
LOVE &
Laundry

KEEP THE
CHANGE

Laundry Recipes

ANIMAL

Mom
Dad

Milo

Linens

Izzy
Abby

Chapter Eight

My Favorite Tips, Tricks and Solutions

I have literally spent years trying just about every organizing tip I have ever stumbled across. It's not just about trying to make my life easier anymore, organizing and re-organizing my home is pretty much my favorite pastime. I often try new systems just for fun (I may need more of a social life).

I've pretty much exhausted Pinterest at this point, and I can't walk by a checkout without scanning the magazines for some new and unique solution I haven't tried yet. Some of the best organizing solutions in my home have actually come out of trial and error (mostly errors), and honestly, the simplest systems are almost always the best.

So now that you have a good foundation and the knowledge needed to become an organizing expert, I'm going to share with you some quick projects that had a

huge impact on my home and my family. **I've picked the best of the best to share with you, the ones that work in real life for real families with real amounts of clutter. No fancy tools required or budget breaking solutions here, just simple tips that really work.**

Landing Strip

The idea of creating a "landing strip" at your front door isn't a new concept. In fact, I have heard this tip so many times I roll my eyes when I read about it in a new organizing book because it is literally in every single one (including this one, cue eye-rolling as I write). Do you know why every single Professional Organizer mentions a landing strip in every single book he or she writes? Because it really is a must-have for every home. The most hilarious thing is, I really only created a proper landing strip about a year ago. I mean, I thought I had a proper place for my keys and purse and other things when I came home, but in truth, there were a few spots they would often end up. To truly have a functional landing strip, you need a hook or container for your keys and other designated places for all the things you set down when you first walk through the door. The top of your kitchen island or tossed onto your table is not a proper landing spot.

For our family, we love this Ikea shoe cabinet. The top drawer has divided bins that hold our keys, wallets, glasses, and spare change. We have a basket on the top of the cabinet for other random things we may drop, like receipts or junk mail. Since we live in Canada and no one wears shoes in the house in Canada, this is also a perfect place to store our shoes.

Create your own landing strip today; it is the perfect way to kick-start your organizing fun and ensure you'll never lose your keys again. Check out Pinterest for a bazillion options for creating the perfect landing strip for your home.

Cord Box

This simple organizing solution was one of the first I ever used, and I am still using it today. I literally just got a medium size container and placed all of my spare cords, cables, and chargers in it. We also store extra extension cords and power bars in this bin as well. Maybe it's just our house, but we have a lot of extra cords! Before the cord box, USB, HDMI, phone cords and so many other random chargers were always left here, there, and everywhere. Now we have a home for all of those cables, and we always know exactly where they are when we need them. I did light micro-organizing inside of our cord box, using separate smaller containers inside for USB cables and another container just for chargers. Let me tell you, the small effort it took to create this bin has saved us countless hours of searching and rummaging.

Kitchen Command Center

I mentioned our Kitchen Command Center in a previous chapter, but the fact that it is super-duper important in keeping a busy family organized made me want to toss it in this list for you again. **Having one central place for a family calendar and place to put notes and reminders is a must-have for every home.** I like using the kitchen because it is where we spend most of our time together as a family. We use the side of our fridge to hold a magnetic family calendar, message board, and a host of to-do lists, as well as our weekly menu. We also have an accordion file folder for important school papers, friends' birthday invitations, extracurricular activity schedules, and so much more.

Choose a convenient spot in your home that can be the command center, and create a space that can help everyone in your family stay organized and on track.

Action File

Paper clutter is always one of the biggest complaints I receive from clients and my followers online. I always recommend creating an action file to store your incoming important papers until you have the time to deal with them properly. In our home, the action file is a magazine rack, which hangs on the wall in our office, so it is really visible for my husband. We have labeled our file folders to be paid, to be filed, to do, and for review. When we bring in the mail or print off an important paper, we place it into the appropriate file folder immediately to avoid the dreaded paper pile trap. No matter what file system you prefer to use, whether it is open baskets, an accordion file folder, or a magazine rack, creating an action file will make paper clutter a thing of the past.

In/Out System

A few years ago I created an in/out system, and now there is no going back! Basically, this is just a few baskets on a shelf in our mudroom, but it really has helped cut down on the random clutter in my home. If you don't have a mudroom, find a little space somewhere near your entrance for your own in/out

system. We have two baskets for donations, one to go to family members and another one for our local thrift store. Having these so easy to access means that when we come across something we are not using, or clothing that no longer fits, we can easily put it immediately into our donation bin. I also have separate donation bins in my kids' closets, because they outgrow clothing seemingly overnight.

The third bin in our in/out system is for things that need to be returned to the store, or library books or things we have borrowed from friends and family. Just having a place to put these things means they are no longer sitting out on the counter, or in a pile on the floor waiting until we have time to return them.

Lastly, I use one bin for the new things coming into our home if I don't have a place to put them right away. These are usually things like decorations for an upcoming birthday party or other items that just don't have a designated place to go yet. Before my in/out system, all of these random things added up to a lot of clutter just laying around my home. If you are short on space, just creating one donation box in your home will really help cut down on clutter and make regular purging much easier.

Contain Condiments

Did you know that most refrigerators have removable bins on the door that are actually designed to store your condiments? I had no idea, and when I discovered how easy it was to take off and put back these bins, I was totally giddy. The simple act of placing all of your condiments into one container in your fridge will save you a crazy amount of time. The best part, besides never having to look for the ketchup again, is that you can easily bring the entire container right to the table (or outside BBQ) and no longer have to struggle with multiple bottles.

We have one container just for salad dressings, one for BBQ sauces, one for condiments, and one for syrups. Let me tell you, not only do we never have to search for anything in the fridge, but we can also carry everything we need over to the table with just one hand! I can't even describe the difference that this tiny fridge-organizing tip will have; you have to try it for yourself.

Gift Closet

I buy Christmas and birthday gifts for my children throughout the year, especially if I find toys I know they will love on sale. I also like buying gifts for friends and family all year long, so the Christmas rush is a little less hectic. The problem with year-long gift buying is having a designated place for those gifts to go in the meantime. I used to hide gifts in really good hiding places around my home. More often than not, I would totally forget where those random hiding places were, or I would forget I had even bought the gifts in the first place.

Enter the gift closet. I had a closet that was literally filled with useless junk in my downstairs bathroom and I decided to transform it into our little gift closet. In the bathroom, yeah, I know, it's weird. Listen, you gotta work with what you have and in this case, I had an empty closet and a really good use for it.

The best part about my little gift closet is that I was able to use one empty shelf just for a wrapping station. Now I have everything I need including wrapping paper, ribbon, cards, gift bags, and even gifts all together and organized in one easy to access space…even if it is in the bathroom.

Cleaning Caddy

You can save a lot of time cleaning your house just by organizing all of the products and tools you regularly use into one easy-to-carry caddy. I picked up my cleaning caddy from the dollar store and filled it with rags, gloves, cleaners, a toothbrush, duster, and scrub brush so that I can quickly move from room to room and have everything I need. So grab a pail or a caddy and organize all of your favorite cleaning supplies together today.

Lost Sock Bag

One of the biggest laundry mistakes I ever made was putting single, lost socks into my sock drawer. I can still remember rummaging through my sock drawer on rushed mornings, trying in vain to find a match. Craziness. Here's the thing, you should never, ever put lonely socks into your sock drawer; it just creates unnecessary work and frustration. I began by emptying my sock drawer and only putting back the paired matches. All of the lonely, unmatched socks went into a bag, my lost sock bag. Whenever I come across a lost sock, I toss it into the bag with the others. Now, here is where the fun part begins! Once a month or so, my family and I empty out the bag into a big pile, and we race to see who can find the most matches. It's actually a pretty fun family game, and my kids and even my husband love to play (pretty sure Joe only likes it because he ALWAYS wins). Trust me, even though this may seem like a boring chore, it can be a fun matching game. It also helps to sing love songs as you find a sock's long lost mate!

DIY Kitchen Pull-Outs

Organizing a kitchen can be a big job, but it doesn't have to be expensive. One of my favorite tips for organizing deep cabinets is to use baking pans or shallow dollar store containers to hold all of your kitchen gadgets. I used to pull everything out of my small appliance cupboard in order to get to the items I needed in the back. Now, I simply slide out the basket or the baking pan, grab what I need, and slide it back in when I am done. If you have ever dreamed of expensive pull-outs for your cabinets, this tip will give you the same results for just $1 per shelf. I also use shallow dollar store containers to corral all of my Tupperware and kids' dishes, making sure cluttered cabinets are a thing of the past.

Homeless Clutter Catchers

No matter how neat and organized your home is, you are still going to have clutter from time to time. A simple solution that will catch incoming clutter is to designate a spot for your homeless clutter in your main living areas. In my kitchen, craft room, living room, and master bedroom, I have pretty baskets whose only job is to hold clutter until I have a chance to deal with it properly.

Sometimes life gets in the way and we just don't have the time to put away or create new homes for everything we bring home. A clutter catching basket is just a temporary spot to place the clutter until you have a chance to put it away. Having a basket or bin for homeless clutter is important, because it can halt the spread across your surfaces. The problem is, clutter attracts more clutter… like a magnet. One little pile of paper on your desk can seem to grow into a mountain almost overnight. When you contain it in a basket, it is far less likely to continue spreading, and it is a great visual reminder to empty the basket when it is full.

Household Management Binder

I talked a little about the importance of a Household Management Binder already once in this book, but it's important enough to bring up again. My binder is so much more than just a place to store cleaning checklists and monthly calendars; it is also a spot to hold all of our important family information. In my binder, I have a section for medical information, which includes my children's immunization records and a detailed medical history for each family member (even our parents). I also have helpful information in case of an emergency, like the contact info for our lawyer and our insurance information, including the policy numbers.

My husband thinks my binder is a little bit overkill and even a tad morbid, but the truth is, if anything every happened to the both of us, our extended family would have everything they need to take over our household in an emergency situation.

Being organized isn't just about having a tidy house, it is also about being prepared for the future. I have peace of mind knowing I have planned and prepared the best I could in the unlikely event I kick the bucket tomorrow.

Memory Bins

One of my biggest clutter struggles in the beginning of my life as a mom was sentimental clutter. You know the kind I'm talking about: your child's first Halloween costume or her first-ever trophy. Don't even get me started on the artwork and photos that can all seem so important to keep. For me, I have to be careful not to keep too much, and I am all too aware of passing on guilty clutter to my children.

In our home, one solution that really works is having a memory bin for each family member. We keep our memory bins in the office closet so they are easy to access when we need them. When my kids bring home their report cards or outgrow a really special outfit I want to keep, I can easily place it into their memory bin right away. I also like having one for my husband and me, because there are often new accomplishes or keepsakes that we have, even as adults.

The best part of having an easy-to-access memory center is that I can easily slip in little notes from time to time as well. I'm not a scrapbooker, and I used to feel bad for not taking the time to create beautiful memory books for my children. A memory bin is so much easier, and I can quickly write sweet notes to them,

like, "Today you got your first goal in hockey and I was so proud of you," and slip them into their box.

One day, when my kids are grown and have little ones of their own, they can go through the box and keep what they like. Having just one box per family member means I can still keep the important stuff, without having to dedicate half of my storage to memories.

These are just a few simple organizing solutions that I think every house should have. They will save you time, effort, and make your busy life just a little less stressful each day. Choose just one of these tips and give it a try for yourself today. For more organizing tips and tricks, you can visit my website at www.clutterbug.me.

Chapter Nine

Organizing for Small Children

Kids can be messy. Trying to clean the house when you have small children can seem like shoveling your driveway in the middle of a snowstorm. If you are overwhelmed by the mess your little ones make, you're not alone. Kids' clutter is one of the biggest issues for most of my clients and online followers.

Contrary to popular belief, you can have kids running around like little tornados and still have a clean and organized home, without having to pick up after them all day-long. Actually, once you have put some of my favorite organizing systems in place, you will never have to pick up toys again! **You may be rolling your eyes right about now, but let me assure you, the right organizing solutions can work miracles in even the most toy-cluttered homes.** Our house is definitely proof of this.

Let's just lay it all out: children come with a ridiculous amount of stuff. Anyone with a newborn can attest to the fact that, despite being the size of a football, babies can fill your home with so many gadgets and gizmos that any resemblance of your grown-up, pre-baby space vanishes before they even come home from the hospital. When my kids were first born, we bought so many contraptions that swung them, rocked them, and vibrated them; my living room barely had room for living. Those giant rainbow-colored jiggling machines were sanity savers in those first few sleep-deprived months of parenthood, but as the baby clutter grew, so did my stress and the dislike of my home.

The landslide of children's items coming into my home didn't stop after infancy either. With three kids growing fast,

buying clothes is a year-round event, and there seems to be a holiday requiring new toys every few months. With three sets of grandparents and six sets of great-grandparents buying my children gifts throughout the year, it didn't take long for my home to become a giant, brightly-colored disaster zone.

Every night I would clean up all their toys, books, and games, just to do it all over again the next day. My life was like the movie Groundhog Day, if only the movie was about a stressed-out, overly-emotional mother who was living in a pile of rainbow-colored junk. I mean, why does everything made for children have to be so loud and so painfully bright? It's a bloody miracle I made it through those years without going completely bonkers. I was desperate for a clean and organized home we could enjoy as a family, not just a fun house for kids aged five and under. The mess was making me miserable, and when Mom is miserable, the entire family is miserable.

I was running a home daycare and at one point, I had nine little ones running around all-day. One of my more...spirited daycare girls used to literally swing from my chandelier, and I felt like I was living in a zoo with tiny mess-making monkeys.

After too many years of stepping on toys and endlessly cleaning, I decided to try different organizing methods to help save what little sanity I had left.

My only organizational goal in the beginning was to spend less time cleaning up the toys every night. **I literally tried every organizing system I could find for kids' toys. I could have built a new house with the wasted toy boxes and plastic containers that never keep the toys organized for very long. When I finally found the holy grail of toy organization, I never had to pick up a random child's toy again (cue the angels singing background music).** Once this system was set up, the playroom became a beautifully clean and tidy toy-topia literally overnight, with no upkeep needed on my part. The best part? Once the toys were organized and easier for the children to find and play with, the kids were so much happier and rarely needed me for entertainment anymore. I know what you're thinking, it may seem unbelievable, but I promise you, my toy-organizing system really is magic. Don't worry, I'm going to cover this life-changing toy-organizing system later in this chapter!

Here's the greatest thing about organizing: **it isn't just about having a pretty or tidy space, it is about making your space so functional that it saves you time, energy, and requires minimal effort to maintain.**

After the toys were organized, I started searching for other ways to set up organizing systems for my kids and my daycare. The new toy system had such a huge impact on everyone that I wanted to keep the momentum going, and the more I organized, the more I began seeing amazing and unexpected results. The kids were happier and way more independent, and I had more time to spend with them than ever before.

A few months after I was running my daycare "like a boss," I had a parent tell me how thrilled she was that I was running a Montessori-style daycare. She gushed about how her friends at a play date were all amazed at how her young toddlers could put on their own coat and shoes, and how they cleaned up after themselves so well. I didn't mention to her that I had no idea what "Montessori method" even was, or that the only reason her children had this newfound independence was because I was tired of doing those things for them. I simply smiled and nodded.

After she left, I did a little Google research on the Montessori method, and I have to say, they are totally onto something. Montessori schools and daycares base their core values on creating environments that teach children to be more independent. Children play independently, clean up independently, and are able to easily master basic life skills that some teenagers can't even do. Organization is key in creating these educational and fun play spaces for children in Montessori-style schools and daycares, and you can easily recreate these systems in your own home, too.

I saw a huge change in both my own children and my daycare children after I had set up new and easy organizing solutions for them. They could put on their own shoes and coats, get their own drinks and snacks, pick up their toys, and sweep and mop the daycare room;because they could easily access everything they wanted and needed, they rarely required any assistance from me.

The results from my daycare efficiency project were incredible. The children were happier, my home was cleaner, and I had so much more time every day. I was no longer a frazzled, overworked stay-at-home mom, and yet I was doing a much better job as a parent than I ever had before. I am going to share a few of my favorite tips and tricks with you when it comes to organization for small children. These little changes can make a huge impact, and they can help your children become happier, tidier, and more independent little humans! So let's get started!

Toys

Let's talk toys! **This toy method works for all small children, and it will ensure that their toys stay clean and organized for good!** Everyone who has tried this method with their children agrees that this simple concept can banish toy clutter for good. First, you must get rid of all of your toy boxes. **Toy boxes just do not work.**

What works for children is a sorted, labeled, open container system. Step one to creating this system is to sort all the toys into similar categories. Make these categories really simple. Here are a few examples: dolls, building blocks, action figures, puzzles, cars, and balls… hopefully you get the idea! **Now place each one of these categories into a container that does not have a lid.** Be sure the container is large enough to hold everything in the category, without having to force the toys inside. You can always create two containers for each category if you have too many for just one container. I love using deep plastic containers from the dollar store or canvas bins for toy storage. Once all of the toys are sorted into bins, clearly label the front of the bins with a large and easy to read label. If your children are too young to read, use picture labels instead.

Once all of your containers are sorted and labeled, place them on low shelving units so that the children can easily get them down and put them back all by themselves.

When you first set up this system, you will need to enforce the one-container-at-a-time rule. This is a temporary rule you need to enforce only until your children become used to picking up the toys from that one container all by themselves. **The rule is: you can only play with one container at a time and you must clean up that container and put it away before you can take out another one.** This will ensure that the mess will never get out of control for your little ones and train them to quickly and easily pick up their toys.

Once you feel your child can move to two or three containers at a time, just remind them not to mix the containers while cleaning up. Only dolls go in the doll bin, only cars in the car bin. Here is why this is important and why this method works: if the toys are sorted, children never have to rummage or dump toys on the floor to find what they

are looking for. It is easier to find what they want and much more fun to play when toys are sorted into categories for them. Of course, it also makes cleaning up easier, too.

My children have been using the sorted toy method for over six years, and I have never had to help them clean or organize their toys since we started using this method. Their bedrooms and the playroom are always clean, and they can easily find everything they want to play with without any help from me.

Toy Rotation

Toy rotation is a must-do in order to keep toy clutter under control. It also has the added benefit of keeping your child way more focused, and it makes playing with old toys seem new and fun again. This simple concept is a lifesaver if your child has a lot of toys. **Once the toys are sorted into separate containers, store half of those containers out of sight.** Dedicate a closet, under a bed, or a spot in a storage area to keep half of your child's toys. We have a toy closet, and once every couple of weeks or so, I rotate those toy bins with the ones currently in their room or play room. I can also pull out a new toy bin whenever I need a quiet minute, and it's always like Christmas morning all over again.

Once the toys are stored out of sight, most children forget all about them. When you bring them out, it's like they are getting brand-new toys all over again, and it reignites their interest in them. If your little one seems bored or is reluctant to self-play, toy rotation is going to be a game changer for you. Here is a "you're welcome" in advance.

Coats And Shoes

Hooks are also a must for small children. You just cannot expect little kids to hang up their coat on a hanger when they come home from school (despite daily nagging). It will almost always end up on the floor. Instead, install hooks either inside the closet or by the door where they can easily hang their coats and backpacks when they get home, while still keeping your home tidy and organized. Be sure to hang hooks at their eye level, so that they can easily reach the hooks. You can also install hooks in their bedroom for pyjamas and other clothing they have worn once, but are not yet dirty enough to go into the wash.

The same idea works for shoes. While we did (and still do) have a closet for shoes and coats, my children rarely took the time to put their shoes away when they got home. By giving them a dedicated shoe basket or cubbies located right by the door, my children could easily put their shoes away as soon as they got home.

The added benefit of being able to say, go get your shoes and coat on, and knowing they can do this without any help from you can save you so much time on those busy and rushed mornings.

Kids' Cupboard

No matter how many children you have, a kids' cupboard in your kitchen is a must-have!

Dedicate one cupboard in your kitchen (a low one that they can easily access) just for your children. You will probably have to do some rearranging for this, and you may have to even get rid of some things in your kitchen that you are not using on a regular basis. While this may be a bit of a hassle, it will be worth it, I promise. **A kids' cupboard is life changing.**

Create a space in your kitchen for your children's cups, plates, utensils, water bottles, and even snacks. Have your children put away their own snacks when you get home from the grocery store (make sure to take the snacks out of the box and store everything in a shallow container in the cupboard). Have them empty their own dishes from the dishwasher and put them away in their cupboard. They can also set the dinner table with their own dishes and get themselves water whenever they are thirsty. When my kids need a snack, they always have to ask first, but they can then help themselves from their own snack cupboard or the fruit and veggie bin in the fridge. Not only does this mean I am no

longer a slave to my little ones' hungry bellies, but I am teaching independence and responsibility for their own belongings. Win, win.

Kids' Clothing

Sometimes you need to do a little more planning and work in the beginning in order to save yourself more time and work later. This is definitely true when it comes to your children's clothing. Nothing is worse than putting away your children's clean clothes only to have them end up on the floor, or back in the dirty hamper before they are even worn. When my little ones turned two, I began teaching them how to dress themselves. Unfortunately, it was much harder than I thought to teach them how to pick out an outfit without making a mess of the clean clothes in the process. My kids would pull clothing from the closet, trying to find the perfect outfit, and leave piles of clean clothes everywhere when they were done. While I was thrilled they were dressing themselves, I was less thrilled to have to rewash, refold, or rehang clothes everyday. The solution? Sorted outfits.

Now when we put away the laundry, we make a few complete outfits for our kids that they can put on quickly and easily all by themselves. For my three-year-old son, we dedicate the bottom drawer of his dresser to outfit pods, which include everything he needs to get dressed every morning. He can still choose what he wants to wear, but we save so much time and stress on busy mornings having

everything bundled together. I lay out a shirt and place folded pants, socks and underwear on top. Then I fold the t-shirt up with everything neatly inside! Every morning he simply picks a pod and gets himself dressed.

My girls are a bit older, so they help me design outfits for the week. We pair pants and a matching shirt together and hang them on the back of their door. On busy mornings, instead of sorting through all their clothing trying to find something to wear, they can choose from the sorted outfits that are ready to go! The time it takes to match outfits saves us so much time on those busy school mornings.

Homework/Art Station

My kitchen island used to be a cluttered mess of crayons, markers, and paper on a regular basis. It was also the spot where my children preferred to do their homework after school while I made dinner. The end result was a constant cluttered mess in my kitchen.

I know I was not alone in this struggle; so many of my clients didn't have a designated space for homework or art in their homes, either.

Creating an organized and efficient workspace for your children can do much more than just keep your home looking neater; a designated homework space, with all of the tools your child would need easily accessible, can help decrease distractions and make doing homework much faster.

Make sure your children's homework or art station is located where they tend to enjoy doing their work now. Empty out a drawer or use a basket to organize everything they need right at their fingertips.

After the birth of our third child, we had to move our two girls into the playroom and make it their shared bedroom. I literally cried over the loss of our beloved playroom, and storing all of their toys in our family room seemed like an impossible feat. My kids have a lot of toys. I'm also a Ladybug, so the idea of transforming our family room into Toy Central gave me heart palpitations.

In the end, it took just one large shelving unit and some new matching bins and baskets to store all of my children's toys and games right in our family room, while still having it look like a clean and clutter-free space.

The loss of our playroom really taught me you could have a fun and tidy toy area in your home, no matter how small of a space you are working with.

A good friend of mine lived in a tiny two-bedroom home with her husband, daughter, and their large dog. Their home was a mere 500 square foot bungalow with no basement or garage, and my friend was forced to embrace tiny living long before it was a hot new trend.

The small living room worked as a place to watch television, eat meals, and as a playroom for their little girl. My friend is not a minimalist by any stretch of the imagination, and still her tiny little home was perfectly organized with a place for everything and everything in its place.

So what was my friend's secret to a tidy, tiny house? The same sorted bin and shelving system that works so well for children's toys was working miracles and keeping everything contained and clutter-free in her small space, too.

So no matter the size of your home or how many toys your family has, you can create a beautiful and clutter-free home that your entire family can enjoy. Having small children doesn't mean you have to live in a space that looks like a toy store after an earthquake. The right organizing system can transform your home and your life, for good.

Chapter Ten

Bloom Where Your Planted

I am guilty of having a bad case of house envy more often than I would like to admit. Beautiful spaces make my heart happy, and more than anything, I want my home to be a beautiful oasis for my family and me to enjoy. Unfortunately, most of those gorgeous, drool-worthy homes I daydream about would cost an absolute fortune to own in reality. I'm not saying I'll never have my dream home, but for now, I need to love the one I have.

Just five years ago, we lived in a tiny 900-square-foot bungalow in a not-so-great part of town. Since I was a little girl, I have always dreamed of living by the water, and I literally spent years checking house listings every single day, trying to find waterfront property we could actually afford. One day, I found the holy grail of houses, a raised ranch in an amazing neighborhood that backed onto a tiny river for a price that seemed too good to be true. We drove to the house with our realtor that same day, and I went directly into the backyard with my husband to see this little river for myself. It was everything I had hoped for, filled with geese and ducks and dozens of their tiny babies swimming in adorable lines. It wasn't just the baby ducks; it was the sound of birds and bugs and flowing water that made the tiny backyard feel like paradise. In that moment, I actually cried. I was determined that we needed to buy this house, no matter what it looked like inside. I was finally home.

I would love to tell you that the inside was as perfect as the little river, but it was far from my dream house. At the time, we only had Izzy and Abby, so with three bedrooms upstairs, the space was perfect. The finishes left something to be desired, though. Everything in the home, while clean and in great shape, was original 1979 décor. The biggest offender was the overabundance of golden oak; it was literally everywhere. The kitchen, the baseboards, the doors, closets, and even the windows were an orangey-golden oak. My first thought was that a little white paint can fix everything, but I kept my negative comments to myself and instead gushed over the house in an attempt to convince my husband that we needed to buy it…like right that second!

We didn't even look at any other houses. We offered the seller asking price that very same day, and were thrilled a few hours later when they accepted it. Our joy was short-lived, though, because the following day they received multiple additional offers over asking price. We were forced to wave all of our conditions in order to secure the deal, which meant no time for a home inspection and no time to sell our current home. Our old house wasn't even on the market yet, and now we owned this one, too!

Despite the fact that my husband and I were both nervous wrecks until our little house was sold, nothing could dampen the excitement over our new home. We ended up selling our home in just four days, and two short months later, that little backyard with the river was ours.

Unfortunately, I couldn't live outside, and the inside of the house quickly started to make me wonder if I had made a hasty mistake. As it turns out, my husband was a fan of golden oak, and was adamant that we would, under no circumstances, ever paint the wood white. I mean, what is it with men and solid wood? Added to the crushing realization I would be permanently living with orange wood and dated bathroom tile, we had a little surprise just a few months after we purchased our home: I was expecting our third baby.

Once our son was born, our three-bedroom home felt as though it was bursting at the seams. Our girls now shared a tiny bedroom, and we had to fill the house with the giant baby-holding devices a new baby requires. Thankfully, our son Milo was the perfect addition to our family, but his arrival left me dreaming of a bigger house.

I really only had two choices at this point: remain resentful of my home, or choose to love it. I chose the second option. With very little money to spend, I decided to make it my mission to love and respect my home as best as I could. The first and most important lesson I learned was that **clean is beautiful.** Every day, I would give my home a "hug" just by keeping it as clean and tidy as I could. As I dusted and vacuumed and tidied my home, I felt myself loving it just a little more every day. **A clean home is beautiful, no matter the décor.**

I also decided to roll up my sleeves and try some inexpensive DIY projects to help make my home a little bit more my style.

Over the past five years and dozens of DIY home projects, I have learned some tips and tricks to make DIYing a success:

- **Start small** – Want to paint your entire kitchen white? Start with the bathroom vanity or a small dresser for practice. Painting, like everything in life, takes some getting used to in order to do it well. By starting on a smaller project, you can learn how best to tackle a big one!

- **A successful DIY project is 90 percent prep** – I had to learn this lesson the hard way, multiple times. Take the time to tape off areas when painting, lay drop clothes, sand properly, and plan your projects ahead of time. Ten minutes of planning and prep work can save you hours of work in the long run!

- **Paint can fix anything** – Ugly tile? You can paint that! Dated furniture? You can paint that! Hideous countertops? Yep…you can even paint those! Paint is a DIYers best friend and can transform any room or any thing on a super small budget.

- **Just go for it** – So many people choose to just live with things in their home they don't love, rather than try and change it for the better. There will always be changes we can't make due to time or budget restraints, but small and easy DIY projects can have a huge impact on your home…and your happiness! Dive right in, no excuses—roll up your sleeves and make a change right now.

My first ever DIY project was our kitchen, which in hindsight was probably not the best spot to practice my handy-woman skills. I loathed that orangey-oak kitchen, and no amount of cleaning could change my feelings. It needed an update, and I needed something easy and budget-friendly.

Compromise was key here. Because my husband was completely against paint-ing the wood white, we agreed I could stain the wood a few shades darker. I bought some gel stain from Amazon and began staining our kitchen while my hus-band was away for work. The end result was much darker than I had originally planned, but I kind of botched the first attempt at staining and so it was a go-dark-or-go-home situation. Needless to say, my husband wasn't impressed, but eventually he came around. **I was able to completely update the entire kitchen with just $60 worth of stain and two cans of silver spray paint for the hardware.**

The end result was a kitchen that, while not perfect, was a space I finally loved. I gel-stained the rest of the oak in my home, a seemingly never-ending pro-cess, and I discovered that with a little sweat equity, I could do a few inexpen-sive updates all by myself.

I'm constantly doing DIY projects now, including painting the tiles in my bathrooms, staining all of the wood in my entire house, installing new floors, refinishing furniture, and so much more. I also have learned to make my own accent pillows and homemade curtains, and just generally make the most with what I have.

Is this now the house of my dreams? Of course not, but I do love and cherish it each and every day. I still wish I could change things, like fix the cracks in the ceiling and drywall the unfinished rooms in the basement, but I try and focus on the positive and make the best of what I have with what I have today.

I'm blooming where I'm planted. I love the saying "bloom where you are planted" so much, I have it printed out and sitting on my desk. It is a daily reminder to me that, no matter what the situation, I need to look at the positive and make the best I can out of it.

My home is dated, but instead of waiting until I have enough money saved for the renovation of my dreams, I am making my home as beautiful as I can with what I have right now. It isn't about spending money on your house; it is about respecting it by keeping it clean and doing small things to make it feel like home.

It is about choosing to love your home just the way it is, and making taking care of it a priority in your life. **It doesn't matter if you own, rent, or still live with your parents; it's about having pride in your surroundings and making your space into a place that brings you joy.**

Of course, I still get house envy when I visit my friend's huge mansion, and I continue to "pin" amazing photos on my "dream home board." The difference is that now, every time I walk in the door, I fall in love with my home just a little more. I make an effort to look at the positive, and I work hard to make it the best it can be.

So, let's stop always waiting for bigger and better. Let's let go of those feelings of house envy that social media can cause. We can make an effort to choose to love and respect our home, each and every day. **When I give my home a great big hug by cleaning and tidying it, a pretty amazing thing happens; my home hugs me back.** A clean and clutter-free home can brighten moods and ease anxiety. A cozy home you find beautiful can wrap you in joy and contentment each time you walk through the front door.

So many of us are guilty of feeling like more can bring us happiness: more money, more stuff, more space, more time. **The truth is, no matter how much we acquire, there will always be so much more we still want.** Being happy with what we have isn't easy; it takes daily effort and self-reminding, but it is so worth it. **We can still have dreams and goals for a bigger and brighter tomorrow, but we need to remember to appreciate and love what we have today.**

I hope I've inspired you to fall in love with your home and treat it with the respect it deserves. Your home is a sanctuary from this hectic world and a place that should make you feel calm and energized, all at the same time. Remember to give your home a daily hug by keeping it clean and clutter-free; it will hug you back every time.

This isn't about how other people will perceive your space. This is for you and your family. If right now your house feels cluttered and overwhelming, don't despair; I've been there, and it won't take long to transform it. Remind yourself that the act of cleaning and de-cluttering is for your own happiness, not a chore to be despised. Treat yourself to a clean and beautiful home today, because you really do deserve it.

Conclusion

If you take only one thing away from this book, I hope like heck it's confidence. Confidence that you can create a beautiful and functional home for you and your family, no matter what state your space is in right now.

You don't have to be a naturally organized person to have an organized home, and you certainly don't have to spend a lot of time or money to make it happen. Consistency is the key. When you schedule just fifteen minutes a day each and every day and dedicate it to de-cluttering and tidying up, you will see a huge impact on your space…and on your life.

While I do hope you now have the urge to purge, I hope more than anything you can now spend less time cleaning your home. Yep, I wrote a book about how to clean and organize your home so you won't have to clean it all the time…oh the irony. The magical part of getting your house organized is that once you've set up the right systems, your housework will immediately be cut in half. Let's face it; no one likes housework.

You can do this. It isn't about having a perfect home, it's about making your life easier. Taking the time to purge and contain your belongings is about freeing yourself up to focus on the things that really matter most to you. Life is short. Let's not waste it looking for lost items, constantly tidying, or feeling anxious in our own homes.

Okay, it's time to get a little philosophical with you now. That was my disclaimer, so brace yourself, because here it comes: **organizing your home will change your entire life.** The way your space looks and functions has a huge impact on the way you feel and the way you and your family function. You will have more time to discover what it is you love to do, and more money to be able to do those things.

Having less clutter means more time with loved ones, more money in your pocket, and way more happiness.

I want you to make a commitment to yourself right now that every day before bed you will spend just fifteen minutes giving your home a great big hug. Hug it by tidying, purging, or organizing just one small space each day. I promise you your home will hug you back, and when it does, you are going to feel amazing.

Acknowledgements

I wrote this book for all of my amazing YouTube subscribers. The love and support I receive from so many of you each and everyday fills me up in a way I can't describe. I love sharing organizing tips with you, but what you give back to me is so much more. You are the reason I am able to do what I love as a career and you are the reason I am able to be home with my children while I do it. I am so grateful for each and every one of you.

I also wanted to thank my wonderful husband Joe. I have no idea what you see in me Joe Man, but I am so blessed that you choose me as your partner. Everything I am and everything I will ever be is because of your support and love. I don't tell you enough (because I don't want it to go to your head) but you are the kindest, funniest and most intelligent person I have ever met.

Of course I have to thank my three incredible kids, Izzy, Abby and Milo. Being your mom is such a joy. Not only are you guys adorable and hilarious, but you make me happier than I ever thought I could be. I am so proud of each of you and no matter where life takes you; I'll always have your back.

I also wanted to give a shout out to Mango Publishing and thank them for taking a chance on me with this book. Working with my editor Hugo has been a pleasure and privilege and it has been an honor to work with the talented Brenda Knight. I also can't forget to thank Peter Walsh for writing the foreword to the book. Peter freaking Walsh! You are my hero and my inspiration, words cannot express my gratitude and the admiration I have for you.

Sometimes wonderful people come into your life and you have no idea how you ever functioned without them. That is the case with the incredibly talented Alice A. Jones. Alice, I am so grateful for your advice, experience and amazing designs.

Lastly, I had to thank my BFF Jessica for always being there for me, even when I get busy and forget to call you for months on end. You get me, you are my person and I love you dude. I also have to thank both my sister-in-law Heather (for helping me make this book less of a hot mess) and my mother-in-law Shelley (for letting me tell the world that you kept your coffee in your bathroom closet ☺). I'm so lucky to have you both as part of my family.

Planner

The first step to any goal is having a plan, and getting organized is no exception. Success in anything we do requires planning and consistency and that is exactly what the planner pages in this book can help you accomplish.

Take a few minutes today to plan your day, week or even month and watch the magic happen. The simple act of writing down your goals will dramatically increase your productivity and motivation.

As a thank you for ordering this book, you can enjoy all of the planner pages in this book as a free instant download from my website.

Simply visit www.clutterbug.me/book and fill out the form on the bottom of the page for your free and exclusive planner pages. Enter the last four digits of the ISBN number on your book (located on the back cover) without any dashes to claim this bonus gift.

Remember, a goal without a plan is just a wish. Make a plan for your biggest goals today and watch them all come true.

ACTION
- NOW -

♡ _____
♡ _____
♡ _____
♡ _____
♡ _____

TODAY'S
- GOALS -

_____
_____
_____
_____

How hard did you
WORK OUT?

◇ ◇ ◇ ◇ ◇

WHAT DID YOU DO?

_____
_____
_____

Chores You need to
Adult today

1 _____
2 _____
3 _____
4 _____
5 _____
6 _____
7 _____
8 _____
9 _____
10 _____

To Do List

○ _____
○ _____
○ _____
○ _____
○ _____
○ _____
○ _____
○ _____
○ _____
○ _____
○ _____
○ _____
○ _____
○ _____
○ _____
○ _____

8oz of water
HYDRATE!

🥛 🥛 🥛 🥛
🥛 🥛 🥛 🥛

OH CRAP
Errands!

1 _____
2 _____
3 _____
4 _____

Eat Balanced
NOM FOODS!

B _____
_____
S _____
L _____
_____
S _____
D _____
_____

Today's
Appointments

1 _____
2 _____
3 _____

MAKE
TODAY
COUNT!

Doodle

NOTES

YOU GOT
THIS!

ACTION
-NOW-

♡ _____
♡ _____
♡ _____
♡ _____
♡ _____

Chores You need to
Adult today

1 _____
2 _____
3 _____
4 _____
5 _____
6 _____
7 _____
8 _____
9 _____
10 _____

OH CRAP
Errands!

1 _____
2 _____
3 _____
4 _____

Today's
Appointments

1 _____
2 _____
3 _____

Doodle

To Do List

○ _____
○ _____
○ _____
○ _____
○ _____
○ _____
○ _____
○ _____
○ _____
○ _____
○ _____
○ _____
○ _____
○ _____
○ _____
○ _____

MAKE TODAY COUNT!

TODAY'S
-GOALS-

_____
_____
_____
_____

How hard did you
WORK OUT?

♢ ♢ ♢ ♢ ♢

WHAT DID YOU DO?
_____
_____
_____

8oz of water
HYDRATE!

Eat Balanced
NOM FOODS!

B _____
_____
S _____
L _____
_____
S _____
D _____

NOTES
YOU GOT THIS!

ACTION
- N O W -

- ♡ _____
- ♡ _____
- ♡ _____
- ♡ _____
- ♡ _____

_____
_____
_____
_____

How hard did you
WORK OUT?

◊ ◊ ◊ ◊ ◊

WHAT DID YOU DO?

_____
_____
_____

Chores You need to
Adult today

1 _____
2 _____
3 _____
4 _____
5 _____
6 _____
7 _____
8 _____
9 _____
10 _____

To Do List

- ○ _____
- ○ _____
- ○ _____
- ○ _____
- ○ _____
- ○ _____
- ○ _____
- ○ _____
- ○ _____
- ○ _____
- ○ _____
- ○ _____
- ○ _____
- ○ _____
- ○ _____
- ○ _____

8oz of water
HYDRATE!

🥛 🥛 🥛 🥛
🥛 🥛 🥛 🥛

Eat Balanced
NOM FOODS!

B _____
_____
S _____
L _____
_____
S _____
D _____
_____

OH CRAP
Errands!

1 _____
2 _____
3 _____
4 _____

Today's
Appointments

1 _____
2 _____
3 _____

MAKE
TODAY
COUNT!

Doodle

NOTES

YOU GOT
THIS!

ACTION
- N O W -

♡ _____
♡ _____
♡ _____
♡ _____
♡ _____

TODAY'S
- G O A L S -

_____
_____
_____
_____

How hard did you
WORK OUT?

○ ○ ○ ○ ○

WHAT DID YOU DO?

_____
_____
_____

Chores You need to
Adult today

1 _____
2 _____
3 _____
4 _____
5 _____
6 _____
7 _____
8 _____
9 _____
10 _____

To Do List

○ _____
○ _____
○ _____
○ _____
○ _____
○ _____
○ _____
○ _____
○ _____
○ _____
○ _____
○ _____
○ _____
○ _____
○ _____
○ _____

8oz of water
HYDRATE!

▯ ▯ ▯ ▯
▯ ▯ ▯ ▯

OH CRAP
Errands!

1 _____
2 _____
3 _____
4 _____

Eat Balanced
NOM FOODS!

B _____
_____
S _____
L _____
_____
S _____
D _____
_____

Today's
Appointments

1 _____
2 _____
3 _____

MAKE
TODAY
COUNT!

Doodle

NOTES

YOU GOT
THIS!

ACTION
- N O W -

♡ _____
♡ _____
♡ _____
♡ _____
♡ _____

_____
_____
_____
_____
_____

How hard did you
WORK OUT?

○ ○ ○ ○ ○

WHAT DID YOU DO?

_____
_____
_____

Chores You need to
Adult today

1 _____
2 _____
3 _____
4 _____
5 _____
6 _____
7 _____
8 _____
9 _____
10 _____

To Do List

○ _____
○ _____
○ _____
○ _____
○ _____
○ _____
○ _____
○ _____
○ _____
○ _____
○ _____
○ _____
○ _____
○ _____
○ _____
○ _____

8oz of water
HYDRATE!

OH CRAP
Errands!

1 _____
2 _____
3 _____
4 _____

Eat Balanced
NOM FOODS!

B _____
_____
S _____
_____
L _____
_____
_____
S _____
_____
D _____
_____
_____

Today's
Appointments

1 _____
2 _____
3 _____

MAKE
TODAY
COUNT!

Doodle

NOTES

YOU GOT
THIS!

ACTION
-NOW-

♡ _____
♡ _____
♡ _____
♡ _____
♡ _____

_____
_____
_____
_____

How hard did you
WORK OUT?

WHAT DID YOU DO?
_____
_____
_____

Chores You need to
Adult today

1 _____
2 _____
3 _____
4 _____
5 _____
6 _____
7 _____
8 _____
9 _____
10 _____

To Do List

○ _____
○ _____
○ _____
○ _____
○ _____
○ _____
○ _____
○ _____
○ _____
○ _____
○ _____
○ _____
○ _____
○ _____
○ _____
○ _____
○ _____

8oz of water
HYDRATE!

OH CRAP
Errands!

1 _____
2 _____
3 _____
4 _____

Eat Balanced
NOM FOODS!

B _____
_____
S _____
L _____
_____
S _____
D _____
_____

Today's
Appointments

1 _____
2 _____
3 _____

MAKE
TODAY
COUNT!

Doodle

NOTES

YOU GOT
THIS!

Daily
PLANNER

Daily
PLANNER

Daily
PLANNER

Daily
PLANNER

Daily
PLANNER

Daily
PLANNER

Weekly
PLANNER

Monday	
Tuesday	
Wednesday	
Thursday	
Friday	
Saturday	
Sunday	

Weekly
PLANNER

CLUTTERBUG

Monday

Tuesday

Wednesday

Thursday

Friday

Saturday

Sunday

Weekly PLANNER

CLUTTERBUG

Monday

Tuesday

Wednesday

Thursday

Friday

Saturday

Sunday

Weekly PLANNER

CLUTTERBUG

Sunday

Saturday

Friday

Thursday

Wednesday

Tuesday

Monday

	Monday
	Tuesday
	Wednesday
	Thursday
	Friday
	Saturday
	Sunday

Weekly
PLANNER

Weekly
PLANNER

CLUTTERBUG

Sunday

Saturday

Friday

Thursday

Wednesday

Tuesday

Monday

Monthly
PLANNER

JANUARY

_____
_____
_____
_____
_____

FEBRUARY

_____
_____
_____
_____
_____

MARCH

_____
_____
_____
_____

APRIL

_____
_____
_____
_____
_____

MAY

_____
_____
_____
_____
_____

JUNE

_____
_____
_____
_____

Monthly
PLANNER

JULY

_____
_____
_____
_____

OCTOBER

_____
_____
_____
_____

AUGUST

_____
_____
_____
_____

NOVEMBER

_____
_____
_____
_____

SEPTEMBER

_____
_____
_____
_____

DECEMBER

_____
_____
_____
_____

Monthly
PLANNER

JANUARY

_____
_____
_____
_____

APRIL

_____
_____
_____
_____

FEBRUARY

_____
_____
_____
_____

MAY

_____
_____
_____
_____

MARCH

_____
_____
_____

JUNE

_____
_____
_____

Monthly
PLANNER

JULY

_____
_____
_____
_____
_____

AUGUST

_____
_____
_____
_____
_____

SEPTEMBER

_____
_____
_____
_____
_____

OCTOBER

_____
_____
_____
_____
_____

NOVEMBER

_____
_____
_____
_____
_____

DECEMBER

_____
_____
_____
_____
_____

Monthly
PLANNER

JANUARY

_____
_____
_____
_____

APRIL

_____
_____
_____
_____

FEBRUARY

_____
_____
_____
_____

MAY

_____
_____
_____
_____

MARCH

_____
_____
_____
_____

JUNE

_____
_____
_____
_____

Monthly
PLANNER

JULY

_____
_____
_____
_____
_____

OCTOBER

_____
_____
_____
_____
_____

AUGUST

_____
_____
_____
_____
_____

NOVEMBER

_____
_____
_____
_____
_____

SEPTEMBER

_____
_____
_____
_____
_____

DECEMBER

_____
_____
_____
_____
_____

Goals For The Week

ME

HONEY DO LIST

Goals For The Week

ME

_____
_____
_____
_____
_____
_____
_____
_____
_____
_____
_____
_____
_____
_____

HONEY DO LIST

_____
_____
_____
_____
_____
_____
_____
_____
_____
_____
_____
_____
_____
_____

Goals For The Week

ME

_____
_____
_____
_____
_____
_____
_____
_____
_____
_____
_____
_____
_____

HONEY DO LIST

_____
_____
_____
_____
_____
_____
_____
_____
_____
_____
_____
_____
_____

Goals For The Week

ME

HONEY DO LIST

Goals For The Week

ME

_____
_____
_____
_____
_____
_____
_____
_____
_____
_____
_____
_____
_____
_____

HONEY DO LIST

_____
_____
_____
_____
_____
_____
_____
_____
_____
_____
_____
_____
_____
_____

Goals For The Week

ME

_____
_____
_____
_____
_____
_____
_____
_____
_____
_____
_____
_____
_____
_____

HONEY DO LIST

_____
_____
_____
_____
_____
_____
_____
_____
_____
_____
_____
_____
_____
_____

My Daily
Cleaning Checklist

Morning

- ◯ Make Beds
- ◯ Empty Dishwasher
- ◯ Clean Kitchen
- ◯ Wipe Bathrooms
- ◯ Plan Day

Evening

- ◯ Load Dishwasher
- ◯ Wipe Kitchen
- ◯ Wipe Bathrooms
- ◯ Pick Up Clutter
- ◯ Put Away Laundry
- ◯ Spot Mop Floors
- ◯ Take Out Garbage

Pick 1 or 2

- ◯ Dust House
- ◯ Mop House
- ◯ Vacuum House
- ◯ Clean Bathrooms
- ◯ Clean Bedrooms
- ◯ Clean Kitchen
- ◯ Declutter
- ◯ Wash Bedding

Once a Month

- ◯ Windows
- ◯ Light Fixtures
- ◯ Baseboards
- ◯ Appliances
- ◯ Picture Frames

My Daily
Cleaning Checklist

Morning
- Make Beds
- Empty Dishwasher
- Clean Kitchen
- Wipe Bathrooms
- Plan Day

Evening
- Load Dishwasher
- Wipe Kitchen
- Wipe Bathrooms
- Pick Up Clutter
- Put Away Laundry
- Spot Mop Floors
- Take Out Garbage

Pick 1 or 2
- Dust House
- Mop House
- Vacuum House
- Clean Bathrooms
- Clean Bedrooms
- Clean Kitchen
- Declutter
- Wash Bedding

Once a Month
- Windows
- Light Fixtures
- Baseboards
- Appliances
- Picture Frames

 CLUTTERBUG

For more printables visit www.clutterbug.me

My Daily
Cleaning Checklist

Morning

- ◯ Make Beds
- ◯ Empty Dishwasher
- ◯ Clean Kitchen
- ◯ Wipe Bathrooms
- ◯ Plan Day

Evening

- ◯ Load Dishwasher
- ◯ Wipe Kitchen
- ◯ Wipe Bathrooms
- ◯ Pick Up Clutter
- ◯ Put Away Laundry
- ◯ Spot Mop Floors
- ◯ Take Out Garbage

Pick 1 or 2

- ◯ Dust House
- ◯ Mop House
- ◯ Vacuum House
- ◯ Clean Bathrooms
- ◯ Clean Bedrooms
- ◯ Clean Kitchen
- ◯ Declutter
- ◯ Wash Bedding

Once a Month

- ◯ Windows
- ◯ Light Fixtures
- ◯ Baseboards
- ◯ Appliances
- ◯ Picture Frames

My Daily
Cleaning Checklist

Morning
- ○ Make Beds
- ○ Empty Dishwasher
- ○ Clean Kitchen
- ○ Wipe Bathrooms
- ○ Plan Day

Evening
- ○ Load Dishwasher
- ○ Wipe Kitchen
- ○ Wipe Bathrooms
- ○ Pick Up Clutter
- ○ Put Away Laundry
- ○ Spot Mop Floors
- ○ Take Out Garbage

Pick 1 or 2
- ○ Dust House
- ○ Mop House
- ○ Vacuum House
- ○ Clean Bathrooms
- ○ Clean Bedrooms
- ○ Clean Kitchen
- ○ Declutter
- ○ Wash Bedding

Once a Month
- ○ Windows
- ○ Light Fixtures
- ○ Baseboards
- ○ Appliances
- ○ Picture Frames

My Daily
Cleaning Checklist

Morning

- ◯ Make Beds
- ◯ Empty Dishwasher
- ◯ Clean Kitchen
- ◯ Wipe Bathrooms
- ◯ Plan Day

Evening

- ◯ Load Dishwasher
- ◯ Wipe Kitchen
- ◯ Wipe Bathrooms
- ◯ Pick Up Clutter
- ◯ Put Away Laundry
- ◯ Spot Mop Floors
- ◯ Take Out Garbage

Pick 1 or 2

- ◯ Dust House
- ◯ Mop House
- ◯ Vacuum House
- ◯ Clean Bathrooms
- ◯ Clean Bedrooms
- ◯ Clean Kitchen
- ◯ Declutter
- ◯ Wash Bedding

Once a Month

- ◯ Windows
- ◯ Light Fixtures
- ◯ Baseboards
- ◯ Appliances
- ◯ Picture Frames

For more printables visit www.clutterbug.me

My Daily
Cleaning Checklist

Morning

- ○ Make Beds
- ○ Empty Dishwasher
- ○ Clean Kitchen
- ○ Wipe Bathrooms
- ○ Plan Day

Evening

- ○ Load Dishwasher
- ○ Wipe Kitchen
- ○ Wipe Bathrooms
- ○ Pick Up Clutter
- ○ Put Away Laundry
- ○ Spot Mop Floors
- ○ Take Out Garbage

Pick 1 or 2

- ○ Dust House
- ○ Mop House
- ○ Vacuum House
- ○ Clean Bathrooms
- ○ Clean Bedrooms
- ○ Clean Kitchen
- ○ Declutter
- ○ Wash Bedding

Once a Month

- ○ Windows
- ○ Light Fixtures
- ○ Baseboards
- ○ Appliances
- ○ Picture Frames

Errands to Run

_____   _____

_____   _____

_____   _____

_____   _____

_____   _____

_____   _____

_____   _____

_____   _____

_____   _____

_____   _____

_____   _____

_____   _____

_____   _____

Errands to Run

_____   _____

_____   _____

_____   _____

_____   _____

_____   _____

_____   _____

_____   _____

_____   _____

_____   _____

_____   _____

_____   _____

_____   _____

_____   _____

_____   _____

Errands to Run

Errands to Run

Errands to Run

Errands to Run

 # For Purchasing

FRESH FRUIT

❑ Apples
❑ Apricots
❑ Bananas
❑ Blueberries
❑ Cherries
❑ Grapefruit
❑ Grapes
❑ Kiwi
❑ Lemons
❑ Limes
❑ Oranges
❑ Peaches
❑ Pears
❑ Pineapple
❑ Plums
❑ Raspberries
❑ Strawberries
❑ Watermelon

FRESH VEGGIES

❑ Avocado
❑ Basil
❑ Broccoli
❑ Carrots
❑ Cauliflower
❑ Celery
❑ Chives
❑ Corn
❑ Cucumber
❑ Garlic
❑ Green Onions
❑ Lettuce

FRESH VEGGIES CONT.

❑ Mushrooms
❑ Onions
❑ Parsley
❑ Potatoes
❑ Spinach
❑ Squash
❑ Thyme
❑ Tomatoes
❑ Zucchini

CONDIMENTS

❑ BBQ Sauce
❑ Oil
❑ Ketchup
❑ Mustard
❑ Mayonaise
❑ Worcestershire Sauce
❑ Hot Sauce
❑ Honey
❑ Salad Dressing
❑ Jam
❑ Miracle Whip
❑ Nutella
❑ Peanut Butter
❑ Plum Sauce
❑ Ranch Dressing

CANNED GOODS

❑ Alfredo Sauce
❑ Applesauce
❑ Baked Beans
❑ Chef Boyardee
❑ Chicken Broth
❑ Fruit
❑ Pasta Sauce
❑ Pickles
❑ Pizza Sauce
❑ Soup
❑ Tomato Paste
❑ Tomatoes
❑ Tuna

DRY GOODS

❑ Bread Crumbs
❑ Cereal
❑ Chocolate Syrup
❑ Cookies
❑ Crackers
❑ Croutons
❑ Dried Fruit
❑ Granola Bars
❑ Jell-O
❑ Oatmeal
❑ Pancake Mix
❑ Pepper
❑ Pudding
❑ Raisins
❑ Salt
❑ Spices
❑ Stuffing

BAKING GOODS

❑ Baking Powder
❑ Baking Soda
❑ Brown Sugar
❑ Brownie Mix
❑ Cake Mix
❑ Chocolate Chips
❑ Cocoa
❑ Corn Starch
❑ Evaporated Milk
❑ Flour
❑ Graham Cracker Crumbs
❑ Icing Sugar
❑ Nuts
❑ Shredded Coconut
❑ Sweetened Condensed Milk
❑ Vanilla Extract
❑ White Sugar

SNACKS

❑ Doritos
❑ Popcorn
❑ Potato Chips
❑ Pretzels
❑ Tortilla Chips

PASTA

- ❏ Egg Noodles
- ❏ Elbow Noodles
- ❏ Kraft Dinner
- ❏ Lasagna Noodles
- ❏ Orzo
- ❏ Spaghetti Noodles

MEAT, FISH, POULTRY

- ❏ Bacon
- ❏ Chicken:
- ❏ Boneless/Bone-In
- ❏ Chicken: Thighs/ Wings
- ❏ Deli Meat
- ❏ Ground Beef
- ❏ Ground Turkey
- ❏ Ham
- ❏ Hot Dogs
- ❏ Pork Chops
- ❏ Pork Loin
- ❏ Roast
- ❏ Salmon
- ❏ Sausage
- ❏ Steak
- ❏ Turkey

DAIRY

- ❏ Butter
- ❏ Cheddar Cheese
- ❏ Coffee Creamer
- ❏ Cream Cheese
- ❏ Dip
- ❏ Eggs
- ❏ Half-n-Half
- ❏ Margarine
- ❏ Milk: Chocolate/ White
- ❏ Mozzarella Cheese
- ❏ Parmesan Cheese
- ❏ Pillsbury Rolls
- ❏ Pillsbury Sweet Rolls
- ❏ Sour Cream
- ❏ Whipped Cream
- ❏ Yogurt

FROZEN

- ❏ French Fries
- ❏ Frozen Fruit
- ❏ Frozen Juice
- ❏ Frozen Veggies
- ❏ Ice-Cream
- ❏ Perogies
- ❏ Pizza
- ❏ Tortellini

BEVERAGES

- ❏ Milk
- ❏ Juice
- ❏ Coffee
- ❏ Water Flavor
- ❏ Juice Boxes
- ❏ Soft Drinks
- ❏ Tea
- ❏ Water

BAKERY

- ❏ Bagels
- ❏ Bread: White/Brown
- ❏ Buns
- ❏ Cookies
- ❏ English Muffins
- ❏ Pie/Dessert
- ❏ Bagette
- ❏ Rolls
- ❏ Tortillas

PAPER PRODUCTS

- ❏ Aluminum Foil
- ❏ Freezer Bags
- ❏ Garbage Bags
- ❏ Paper Towels
- ❏ Parchment Paper
- ❏ Plastic Wrap
- ❏ Sandwich Bags
- ❏ Toilet Paper

CLEANING SUPPLIES

- ❏ Bleach
- ❏ Clorox Wipes
- ❏ Dish Soap
- ❏ Fabric Softener
- ❏ Furniture Polish
- ❏ Glass Cleaner
- ❏ Laundry Detergent
- ❏ Stain Remover
- ❏ Dishwasher Tablets
- ❏ Toilet Bowl Cleaner

PERSONAL CARE

- ❏ Bath Soap/Body Wash
- ❏ Conditioner
- ❏ Deodorant
- ❏ Hairspray
- ❏ Makeup
- ❏ Q-Tips
- ❏ Razors
- ❏ Shampoo
- ❏ Shaving Cream
- ❏ Toothpaste
- ❏ _____

Other

- ❏ _____
- ❏ _____
- ❏ _____
- ❏ _____

 # For Purchasing

FRESH FRUIT
- ❏ Apples
- ❏ Apricots
- ❏ Bananas
- ❏ Blueberries
- ❏ Cherries
- ❏ Grapefruit
- ❏ Grapes
- ❏ Kiwi
- ❏ Lemons
- ❏ Limes
- ❏ Oranges
- ❏ Peaches
- ❏ Pears
- ❏ Pineapple
- ❏ Plums
- ❏ Raspberries
- ❏ Strawberries
- ❏ Watermelon

FRESH VEGGIES
- ❏ Avocado
- ❏ Basil
- ❏ Broccoli
- ❏ Carrots
- ❏ Cauliflower
- ❏ Celery
- ❏ Chives
- ❏ Corn
- ❏ Cucumber
- ❏ Garlic
- ❏ Green Onions
- ❏ Lettuce

FRESH VEGGIES CONT.
- ❏ Mushrooms
- ❏ Onions
- ❏ Parsley
- ❏ Potatoes
- ❏ Spinach
- ❏ Squash
- ❏ Thyme
- ❏ Tomatoes
- ❏ Zucchini

CONDIMENTS
- ❏ BBQ Sauce
- ❏ Oil
- ❏ Ketchup
- ❏ Mustard
- ❏ Mayonaise
- ❏ Worcestershire Sauce
- ❏ Hot Sauce
- ❏ Honey
- ❏ Salad Dressing
- ❏ Jam
- ❏ Miracle Whip
- ❏ Nutella
- ❏ Peanut Butter
- ❏ Plum Sauce
- ❏ Ranch Dressing

CANNED GOODS
- ❏ Alfredo Sauce
- ❏ Applesauce
- ❏ Baked Beans
- ❏ Chef Boyardee
- ❏ Chicken Broth
- ❏ Fruit
- ❏ Pasta Sauce
- ❏ Pickles
- ❏ Pizza Sauce
- ❏ Soup
- ❏ Tomato Paste
- ❏ Tomatoes
- ❏ Tuna

DRY GOODS
- ❏ Bread Crumbs
- ❏ Cereal
- ❏ Chocolate Syrup
- ❏ Cookies
- ❏ Crackers
- ❏ Croutons
- ❏ Dried Fruit
- ❏ Granola Bars
- ❏ Jell-O
- ❏ Oatmeal
- ❏ Pancake Mix
- ❏ Pepper
- ❏ Pudding
- ❏ Raisins
- ❏ Salt
- ❏ Spices
- ❏ Stuffing

BAKING GOODS
- ❏ Baking Powder
- ❏ Baking Soda
- ❏ Brown Sugar
- ❏ Brownie Mix
- ❏ Cake Mix
- ❏ Chocolate Chips
- ❏ Cocoa
- ❏ Corn Starch
- ❏ Evaporated Milk
- ❏ Flour
- ❏ Graham Cracker Crumbs
- ❏ Icing Sugar
- ❏ Nuts
- ❏ Shredded Coconut
- ❏ Sweetened Condensed
- ❏ Milk
- ❏ Vanilla Extract
- ❏ White Sugar

SNACKS
- ❏ Doritos
- ❏ Popcorn
- ❏ Potato Chips
- ❏ Pretzels
- ❏ Tortilla Chips

PASTA

- ❏ Egg Noodles
- ❏ Elbow Noodles
- ❏ Kraft Dinner
- ❏ Lasagna Noodles
- ❏ Orzo
- ❏ Spaghetti Noodles

MEAT, FISH, POULTRY

- ❏ Bacon
- ❏ Chicken:
- ❏ Boneless/Bone-In
- ❏ Chicken: Thighs/ Wings
- ❏ Deli Meat
- ❏ Ground Beef
- ❏ Ground Turkey
- ❏ Ham
- ❏ Hot Dogs
- ❏ Pork Chops
- ❏ Pork Loin
- ❏ Roast
- ❏ Salmon
- ❏ Sausage
- ❏ Steak
- ❏ Turkey

DAIRY

- ❏ Butter
- ❏ Cheddar Cheese
- ❏ Coffee Creamer
- ❏ Cream Cheese
- ❏ Dip
- ❏ Eggs
- ❏ Half-n-Half
- ❏ Margarine
- ❏ Milk: Chocolate/ White
- ❏ Mozzarella Cheese
- ❏ Parmesan Cheese
- ❏ Pillsbury Rolls
- ❏ Pillsbury Sweet Rolls
- ❏ Sour Cream
- ❏ Whipped Cream
- ❏ Yogurt

FROZEN

- ❏ French Fries
- ❏ Frozen Fruit
- ❏ Frozen Juice
- ❏ Frozen Veggies
- ❏ Ice-Cream
- ❏ Perogies
- ❏ Pizza
- ❏ Tortellini

BEVERAGES

- ❏ Milk
- ❏ Juice
- ❏ Coffee
- ❏ Water Flavor
- ❏ Juice Boxes
- ❏ Soft Drinks
- ❏ Tea
- ❏ Water

BAKERY

- ❏ Bagels
- ❏ Bread: White/Brown
- ❏ Buns
- ❏ Cookies
- ❏ English Muffins
- ❏ Pie/Dessert
- ❏ Bagette
- ❏ Rolls
- ❏ Tortillas

PAPER PRODUCTS

- ❏ Aluminum Foil
- ❏ Freezer Bags
- ❏ Garbage Bags
- ❏ Paper Towels
- ❏ Parchment Paper
- ❏ Plastic Wrap
- ❏ Sandwich Bags
- ❏ Toilet Paper

CLEANING SUPPLIES

- ❏ Bleach
- ❏ Clorox Wipes
- ❏ Dish Soap
- ❏ Fabric Softener
- ❏ Furniture Polish
- ❏ Glass Cleaner
- ❏ Laundry Detergent
- ❏ Stain Remover
- ❏ Dishwasher Tablets
- ❏ Toilet Bowl Cleaner

PERSONAL CARE

- ❏ Bath Soap/Body Wash
- ❏ Conditioner
- ❏ Deodorant
- ❏ Hairspray
- ❏ Makeup
- ❏ Q-Tips
- ❏ Razors
- ❏ Shampoo
- ❏ Shaving Cream
- ❏ Toothpaste
- ❏ _____

Other

- ❏ _____
- ❏ _____
- ❏ _____
- ❏ _____

 # For Purchasing

FRESH FRUIT

- ❑ Apples
- ❑ Apricots
- ❑ Bananas
- ❑ Blueberries
- ❑ Cherries
- ❑ Grapefruit
- ❑ Grapes
- ❑ Kiwi
- ❑ Lemons
- ❑ Limes
- ❑ Oranges
- ❑ Peaches
- ❑ Pears
- ❑ Pineapple
- ❑ Plums
- ❑ Raspberries
- ❑ Strawberries
- ❑ Watermelon

FRESH VEGGIES

- ❑ Avocado
- ❑ Basil
- ❑ Broccoli
- ❑ Carrots
- ❑ Cauliflower
- ❑ Celery
- ❑ Chives
- ❑ Corn
- ❑ Cucumber
- ❑ Garlic
- ❑ Green Onions
- ❑ Lettuce

FRESH VEGGIES CONT.

- ❑ Mushrooms
- ❑ Onions
- ❑ Parsley
- ❑ Potatoes
- ❑ Spinach
- ❑ Squash
- ❑ Thyme
- ❑ Tomatoes
- ❑ Zucchini

CONDIMENTS

- ❑ BBQ Sauce
- ❑ Oil
- ❑ Ketchup
- ❑ Mustard
- ❑ Mayonaise
- ❑ Worcestershire Sauce
- ❑ Hot Sauce
- ❑ Honey
- ❑ Salad Dressing
- ❑ Jam
- ❑ Miracle Whip
- ❑ Nutella
- ❑ Peanut Butter
- ❑ Plum Sauce
- ❑ Ranch Dressing

CANNED GOODS

- ❑ Alfredo Sauce
- ❑ Applesauce
- ❑ Baked Beans
- ❑ Chef Boyardee
- ❑ Chicken Broth
- ❑ Fruit
- ❑ Pasta Sauce
- ❑ Pickles
- ❑ Pizza Sauce
- ❑ Soup
- ❑ Tomato Paste
- ❑ Tomatoes
- ❑ Tuna

DRY GOODS

- ❑ Bread Crumbs
- ❑ Cereal
- ❑ Chocolate Syrup
- ❑ Cookies
- ❑ Crackers
- ❑ Croutons
- ❑ Dried Fruit
- ❑ Granola Bars
- ❑ Jell-O
- ❑ Oatmeal
- ❑ Pancake Mix
- ❑ Pepper
- ❑ Pudding
- ❑ Raisins
- ❑ Salt
- ❑ Spices
- ❑ Stuffing

BAKING GOODS

- ❑ Baking Powder
- ❑ Baking Soda
- ❑ Brown Sugar
- ❑ Brownie Mix
- ❑ Cake Mix
- ❑ Chocolate Chips
- ❑ Cocoa
- ❑ Corn Starch
- ❑ Evaporated Milk
- ❑ Flour
- ❑ Graham Cracker Crumbs
- ❑ Icing Sugar
- ❑ Nuts
- ❑ Shredded Coconut
- ❑ Sweetened Condensed
- ❑ Milk
- ❑ Vanilla Extract
- ❑ White Sugar

SNACKS

- ❑ Doritos
- ❑ Popcorn
- ❑ Potato Chips
- ❑ Pretzels
- ❑ Tortilla Chips

PASTA

- ❑ Egg Noodles
- ❑ Elbow Noodles
- ❑ Kraft Dinner
- ❑ Lasagna Noodles
- ❑ Orzo
- ❑ Spaghetti Noodles

MEAT, FISH, POULTRY

- ❑ Bacon
- ❑ Chicken:
- ❑ Boneless/Bone-In
- ❑ Chicken: Thighs/ Wings
- ❑ Deli Meat
- ❑ Ground Beef
- ❑ Ground Turkey
- ❑ Ham
- ❑ Hot Dogs
- ❑ Pork Chops
- ❑ Pork Loin
- ❑ Roast
- ❑ Salmon
- ❑ Sausage
- ❑ Steak
- ❑ Turkey

DAIRY

- ❑ Butter
- ❑ Cheddar Cheese
- ❑ Coffee Creamer
- ❑ Cream Cheese
- ❑ Dip
- ❑ Eggs
- ❑ Half-n-Half
- ❑ Margarine
- ❑ Milk: Chocolate/ White
- ❑ Mozzarella Cheese
- ❑ Parmesan Cheese
- ❑ Pillsbury Rolls
- ❑ Pillsbury Sweet Rolls
- ❑ Sour Cream
- ❑ Whipped Cream
- ❑ Yogurt

FROZEN

- ❑ French Fries
- ❑ Frozen Fruit
- ❑ Frozen Juice
- ❑ Frozen Veggies
- ❑ Ice-Cream
- ❑ Perogies
- ❑ Pizza
- ❑ Tortellini

BEVERAGES

- ❑ Milk
- ❑ Juice
- ❑ Coffee
- ❑ Water Flavor
- ❑ Juice Boxes
- ❑ Soft Drinks
- ❑ Tea
- ❑ Water

BAKERY

- ❑ Bagels
- ❑ Bread: White/Brown
- ❑ Buns
- ❑ Cookies
- ❑ English Muffins
- ❑ Pie/Dessert
- ❑ Bagette
- ❑ Rolls
- ❑ Tortillas

PAPER PRODUCTS

- ❑ Aluminum Foil
- ❑ Freezer Bags
- ❑ Garbage Bags
- ❑ Paper Towels
- ❑ Parchment Paper
- ❑ Plastic Wrap
- ❑ Sandwich Bags
- ❑ Toilet Paper

CLEANING SUPPLIES

- ❑ Bleach
- ❑ Clorox Wipes
- ❑ Dish Soap
- ❑ Fabric Softener
- ❑ Furniture Polish
- ❑ Glass Cleaner
- ❑ Laundry Detergent
- ❑ Stain Remover
- ❑ Dishwasher Tablets
- ❑ Toilet Bowl Cleaner

PERSONAL CARE

- ❑ Bath Soap/Body Wash
- ❑ Conditioner
- ❑ Deodorant
- ❑ Hairspray
- ❑ Makeup
- ❑ Q-Tips
- ❑ Razors
- ❑ Shampoo
- ❑ Shaving Cream
- ❑ Toothpaste
- ❑ _____

Other

- ❑ _____
- ❑ _____
- ❑ _____
- ❑ _____

Published by Mango Publishing Group,
a division of Mango Media Inc.

Cover: Marija Lijeskic
Layout & Design: Nicola DosSantos

Cover photo by © shutterstock.com/Africa Studio

Pages 50, 77, 84, 89, 90, 91, 110, 146: Chad Barry
Photography

Page 11: Melissa Doyle Casting Memories

Page 4: © istockphoto.com/drewhadley
Stock vector ID: 618621260

Page 15: © istockphoto.com/bagi1998
Stock vector ID: 171240376

Page 20: © istockphoto.com/Oko_SwanOmurphy
Stock vector ID: 468046770

Page 25: © istockphoto.com/OGphoto
Stock vector ID: 136185474

Page 29: © istockphoto.com/dangdumrong
Stock vector ID: 171152080

Page 32: © istockphoto.com/macroworld
Stock vector ID: 182782117

Page 33: © istockphoto.com/Spiderplay
Stock vector ID: 178952317

Page 36: © istockphoto.com/MirekKijewski
Stock vector ID: 106462911

Page 38: © istockphoto.com/mapodile
Stock vector ID: 511933338

Page 46: © istockphoto.com/eurobanks
Stock vector ID: 133913415

Page 100: © istockphoto.com/didesign021
Stock vector ID: 495798916

Page 125: © istockphoto.com/RG-vc
Stock vector ID: 164941687

Page 126: © istockphoto.com/KatarzynaBialasiewicz
Stock vector ID: 496479420

Pages 2, 7, 34, 92, 137: © shutterstock.com/Africa Studio
Stock vector IDs: 455538976; 247140583; 134432759;
158765489; 130722767

Pages 138, 144: © shutterstock.com/PopTika
Stock vector IDs: 283925984; 263663474

Page 16: © shutterstock.com/kimson
Stock vector ID: 151302749

Page 96: © shutterstock.com/Joy Brown
Stock vector ID: 19099378

Page 150: © shutterstock.com/conejota
Stock vector ID: 221601982

Page 94: © shutterstock.com/Delpixel
Stock vector ID: 243155815

Page 18: © shutterstock.com/monika3steps
Stock vector ID: 255171361

Page 98: © shutterstock.com/LesPalenik
Stock vector ID: 273326015

Page 126: © shutterstock.com/Photographee.eu
Stock vector ID: 287913881

Page 55: © shutterstock.com/Melpomene
Stock vector ID: 351275555

Page 52: © shutterstock.com/Iulian Valentin
Stock vector ID: 439342990

Eat That Frog, 3rd Edition cover courtesy of
Berrett Koehler Publishers

For permission requests, please contact
the publisher at:

Mango Publishing Group
2850 Douglas Road, 3rd Floor
Coral Gables, FL 33134 USA
info@mango.bz

For special orders, quantity sales, course adoptions and
corporate sales, please email the publisher at sales@
mango.bz. For trade and wholesale sales, please
contact Ingram Publisher Services at customer.service@
ingramcontent.com or +1.800.509.4887.

Real Life Organizing: Clean and Clutter-Free in 15 Minutes
a Day

Library of Congress Cataloging-in-Publication has been
applied for.

ISBN: (paperback) 978-1-63353-519-0, (ebook)
978-1-63353-545-9

BISAC category code HOM005000 HOUSE & HOME /
Do-It-Yourself

Printed in the United States of America